SKEPTICISM, RULES,
AND PRIVATE LANGUAGES

Skepticism, Rules, and Private Languages

Patricia H. Werhane

Humanities Press
New Jersey ▼ London

First published 1992 by Humanities Press International, Inc.,
Atlantic Highlands, New Jersey 07716, and
3 Henrietta Street, Covent Garden, London WC2E 8LU

©1992 by Patricia H. Werhane

Library of Congress Cataloging-in-Publication Data
Werhane, Patricia Hogue.
Skepticism, rules, and private languages / Patricia H. Werhane.
p.   cm.
Includes bibliographical references and index.
ISBN 0-391-03750-1
1. Wittgenstein, Ludwig, 1889–1951. Philosophische
Untersuchungen.   2. Language and languages—Philosophy.
3. Semantics (Philosophy)   I. Title.
B3376.W563P637 1992
401—dc20   91–38783
CIP

A catalog record for this book is available from the British Library

Printed in the United States of America

for my parents
Ruth and Denney Hogue

Contents

Preface

Some time ago one of my colleagues at the American College of Switzerland asked, "But where is your *book* on Wittgenstein?" So at long last this is the book. One may wonder whether there needs to be another book on the later Wittgenstein. But the project of this work is not so much an essay on the *Philosophical Investigations* as it is a development of Wittgensteinian thought, particularly in light of the plethora of secondary literature on this text. Such a project illustrates the richness of Wittgensteinian thought, which allows one to continue to develop fresh interpretations, revise earlier readings, and discover new insights that are important philosophical contributions in their own right.

The book has profited from discussions and comments on various sections by Ardis Collins, Bernard Gert, Jaakko Hintikka, Arnold Levison, Paul Moser, David Ozar, Joseph Pirri, Corliss Swain, and a variety of anonymous readers of chapters of the text. I wish to thank Loyola University of Chicago for an administrative leave which enabled me to start this task; I am indebted to Ronald Walker, Executive Vice President, Lawrence Biondi, S.J., Thomas Bennett, Director of Research Services, and John Bannan, Chairperson, Department of Philosophy, for their support. Ann Dolinko helped to prepare and correct the references, and Cynthia Rudolph provided secretarial assistance, invaluable and thankless work for which I am most grateful.

Acknowledgments

Earlier versions of four of the chapters in this book have been published previously. Parts of Chapter 4 were printed in *Metaphilosophy* 20 (1989): 134–151 under the title, "Does '"Obeying a rule" is a practice' Imply a Community View of Language?" Chapter 5 originally appeared as "Some Paradoxes in Kripke's Interpretation of Wittgenstein," in *Synthese* 73 (1987): 253–273. Chapter 7 was published under the title, "The Constitutive Nature of Rules," in the *Southern Journal of Philosophy* 25 (1987): 239–254, and an earlier version of Chapter 8 appears in the same journal (27 [1989]: 297–314) under the title, "Must We 'Always Get Rid of the Idea of the Private Object'?" The discussion of moral realism in Chapter 4 is part of an extended analysis of this topic in "Wittgenstein and Moral Realism," *Journal of Value Inquiry* 26 (1992). I thank these journals for permission to reprint revised versions of these articles.

Introduction

In the *Philosophical Investigations* Ludwig Wittgenstein defines a private language as follows:

> . . . [t]he individual words of this language are to refer to what can only be known to the person speaking; to his immediate private sensations. So another person cannot understand the language.[1]

The possibility of a language that is incomprehensible to anyone but its speaker may seem strange to contemporary readers who have been brought up on the idea that languages are inherently social. Language, as the means of expression and communication, appears only in a social context. Every human community has a well-developed language, although not always a written one, and there is only negative evidence that people brought up in isolation from a human community learn to speak on their own.[2]

At the same time, each of us finds it at least intuitively evident that we have sensations, feelings, intentions, ideas, dreams, and even images that are felt, perceived, or experienced by ourselves alone. Most of us would concur that ordinarily the meanings of words referring to these kinds of experiences and the referring words themselves are comprehensible to persons other than the one who undergoes the experience. Yet these sorts of experiences appear to be private, or, minimally, the "objects" of these experiences, such as dreams, pains, and images, appear to be available only to the person experiencing them and not shared or shareable in any ordinary perceptual ways. How is it then that the language one uses to refer to and denote these phenomena is not? The problem is not merely that the objects of reference words denoting these phenomena are in some sense private, but that the meanings of terms referring to experiences not perceivable to others might themselves be derived privately as well. So either one cannot make sense of privately experienced phenomena on the basis of their alleged private references or privately derived meaning, or the language one formulates to talk about these phenomena is in some sense a private language.

Historically, the idea of a private language has had import in certain schemes in which philosophers have tried to carry out a philosophical

1

analysis starting from private or personal experiences. Such an analysis often begins from what is claimed to be an indubitable starting point, such as Descartes' well-known *cogito* or one's immediate, unquestionably present sensations. David Hume's analysis of the idea of "impression" as he presents this idea in *A Treatise of Human Nature* may be an example of the latter. In the beginning of the *Treatise* Hume declares, "nothing is ever present to the mind but perceptions."[3] Many of these perceptions are impressions, indubitable but fleeting individual idiolectic sense data which, according to Hume, constitute the basis of our perceptions, ideas, and knowledge. In fact, we are certain only about the existence and nature of our private impressions, despite their ephemeral nature. If individual impressions are the sole basis for philosophical inferences, then each person's language is developed from an idiosyncratic idiolect, and knowledge is derived and inferred from private impressions and only from these data. The issue of whether the language I develop from my impressions has any relation to yours is impossible to resolve, because there is no way to verify that the set of personal impressions out of which I create a language has any parallels to your set of impressions. Nor has one any means to judge whether my use of words such as "pain," for example, is the same or different from your use of such sounds. Such a language so developed might, then, be a private language, comprehensible only to its speaker.

Arguments purporting to show that a private language is impossible, commonly called the "private language arguments," were developed by Wittgenstein and others at least in part to meet the difficulties of a Humean kind of approach. In outline, these arguments, in their original form, were constructed as follows. First, one tries to develop a language merely from making sound-sensation associations from what supposedly are one's own private experiences such as immediate sensations or impressions. Second, since one has only impressions or sensations out of which to construct a language, sound-object associations are made, in the first instance, privately by ostensive definitions. But third, under these limited conditions the means for making consistent word-object associations and correcting one's errors are necessarily not available. So the "language" one creates under these circumstances is not a language at all. A philosophical analysis that attempts to derive its principles and theses merely from the starting point of a private experience must do so by ostensive definition. Therefore any such project is necessarily doomed to failure from its inception.

If the original private language arguments are valid, they are of crucial philosophical importance. The arguments bring into question the centrality of ostension or at least private ostensive definition, as the starting place for reference, language, and philosophical analysis. Their conclusions also challenge a number of forms of solipsism. According to the private language arguments, even if one could derive a language privately, the language would be comprehensible to others. A philosophical analysis that begins from an allegedly indubitable private experience such as an impression or the *cogito* is already conceived and defined in a language understandable to others. Thus to defend a solipsistic position one has to do so in a language that is *not* solipsistic.

The private language arguments also bring into question certain claims of linguistic relativism. At least some linguistic relativists argue that not all languages are translatable or comprehensible to each other. Even so-called translations of one language into another are, at best, incomplete, since most terms in a particular language do not have their conceptual equivalents in another. Thus many concepts in one language are incommensurable with concepts in another. In principle, then, one cannot always understand ideas that are "essentially different from our own."[4] But if the notion of a private language makes no sense, then it is not merely the case that a person by herself could not develop a language that was incomprehensible. The logical possibility of concepts that are in principle incommensurable is challenged as well.

Linguistic relativism is related to another thesis, that of linguistic idealism. A linguistic idealist argues that the meanings of terms and the ways in which language supposedly refers to the world are "*created* by grammar."[5] So, for example, color terms in English are not merely examples of a particular set of conventions that express a kind of relationship between sense perceptions and their objects, so that "red," for example, is a way, in English, adopted to refer to, and corresponds with, perceived colors in nature. Rather, the concept of color, the notion of a colored object, and acts of referring are "*created* by grammar." The fact that we identify colors, for example, is a convention, and the claim that nature is "colored" is itself not a truth but an assertion created by conventions.[6] It is sometimes argued, as we shall see, that the private language arguments result in a sort of linguistic idealism. If a language cannot be derived privately from sound-sensation ostensive associations, then, it is concluded, languages develop out of community consensus, a consensus which is merely a matter of agreement or habit. Moreover, if references cannot be established in the first instance by ostensive sound-phenomenon associations, references are merely assertive devices created out of societal habits and dispositions. So "red" is not a word in English that enables us to refer to colors in nature, but rather, that we perceive coloredly and identify that alleged fact linguistically is itself a matter of consensus for which there is no independent justification or verification.

This conventionalist rendering of the private language arguments is one of a number of post-Wittgensteinian contemporary reformulations of these claims. Each of these reformulations focuses on a particular dimension of the notion of a private language, each prompts a reinterpretation of the consequences of the private language arguments, and each introduces new philosophical outcomes. According to one popular revisionist version of the private language arguments, a position I shall call a Community View (or Views),

> Wittgenstein's point [in the private language arguments] . . . is a . . . radical one, that what it is for a person to be following a rule, even individually, cannot ultimately be explained without reference to some community.[7]

This perspective concerns itself with the question of whether a language could develop in social or linguistic isolation. Such a thesis argues that the impossibility of a private language implies that language evolves only within a community. Languages, grammar, and language rules are social conventions derived from, and dependent upon, social practices. Thus a language could not in fact or in theory be created by someone in physical or linguistic isolation from a community of other human beings.

There are different versions of a Community View. Some of its proponents hold that "[t]he general practice of the community is constitutive of its linguistic rules."[8] Others extend the analysis to derive a form of antirealist linguistic idealism. Because a language cannot be developed from an ostensive idiolect, rule-following and thus language conventions and grammar are indeterminate, evolving from a sort of arbitrary "cottoning on" to certain practices, adopted willy-nilly by community consensus as "correct" rules for going on.[9]

That the private language arguments commit one to a form of relativism, conventionalism, linguistic idealism, and/or antirealism has significant philosophical consequences. The thesis that language develops arbitrarily and that language conventions are indeterminate is a conclusion that challenges the heart of rationality and commonsense beliefs. But this conclusion is itself subject to question. Community consensus, strong as it may be, does not preclude a certain determinacy in language rules and the uses of words. Moreover, some Community Views confuse the fact that isolated human beings do not develop a language with the logical impossibility of this occurrence. Although its proponents claim that their arguments eliminate the intelligibility of language development in isolation, the fact that a community derives a language from its habits and dispositions is not strong enough evidence to preclude that possibility of a single person making such derivations as well. Community Views do not solve the problem of linguistic relativism either, since heterogeneous communities could develop distinct languages that were incomprehensible to each other, thus establishing private languages on a macro level.

Controversies over how one should interpret the private language arguments have been spurred on with the publication of Saul Kripke's book, *Wittgenstein on Rules and Private Language*. Kripke sees Wittgenstein's interest in the private language arguments as part of a larger project in which Wittgenstein responds to the skeptic's paradox that "no course of action could be determined by a rule, because every course of action can be made to accord with the rule."[10] Kripke argues that language develops from the brute fact of primitive prelinguistic agreements in reactions. Conventions or rules are nothing more than assertions based on these expressions of agreement. Each attempt by an individual to follow a rule or to follow it consistently is merely another form of an intention or assertion to grasp the rule. Since there are no independent criteria for rule-following apart from these assertions, one can never know if one is following the same rule or following a rule correctly. This argument results in a radical rule-skepticism, a skepticism that extends to truth-conditions and thus to rationality itself. So-called rules are merely arbitrary assertions based on brute agreements that themselves cannot be independently verified. Truth conditions are merely assertability conditions, and what we call "knowledge" is based on these assertions.

Kripke's very carefully crafted reasoning, like that of the Community Views, leaves open the possibility of alien languages that are incommensurable with our own. Moreover, his analysis of intention is reminiscent of Hume's. Kripke needlessly postulates a realist theory of intentions, a postulation that raises a number of difficulties such that one then has to make sense of intentions as mental states from which allegedly nonprivate language is derived.

In the evolution of the private language arguments, the term "privacy" itself has a number of possible definitions, each of which influ-

ences the kinds of claims being proposed by the private language arguments and, indeed, the nature of so-called private experiences themselves. The first formulations of the private language arguments focused
on the possible subject matter for such a language, immediate private
sensations. The term "private" could be defining a phenomenon that is
in fact experienced, comprehended, or available only to one person, or it
could be defining a phenomenon that is in principle experienceable or
intelligible only by one person. Similarly, a private language could be a
language that is incomprehensible in fact *or* in principle to anyone but its
speaker. Its privacy could be due to the private references of its words or
to its construction, rules, and grammar. It could be a language that is
developed in social or linguistic isolation from others, or merely a
personal language derived from another language. What one means by
a private experience or a private language, in turn, affects the substance
of the subsequent analysis and the conclusions elicited from such arguments. Community Views, which focus on the question of linguistic and
physical isolation, result in a form of linguistic relativism. Kripke's
rule-skepticism raises questions about the nature of truth and reality.

The original private language arguments are sometimes thought to
demonstrate that the notion of a necessarily private (mental) phenomenon makes no sense. If a language cannot be developed from
private ostensive definitions, it is difficult to explain how it is that we
can refer to and speak about phenomena such as one's impressions,
pains, dreams, or even thoughts, phenomena that are supposedly experienced or available to one person, because there are no private
criteria for that identification. If such reference is impossible, and if the
meanings of sensation and psychological terms are nonprivate, it is
sometimes thought that accepting the private language arguments commits one to a form of logical behaviorism about sensations and psychological phenomena, since one cannot refer to these phenomena except
with terms whose meanings are publicly derived.

One of the reasons for various revisionary attempts at reformulating
the private language arguments is to explain Wittgenstein's ubiquitous
expression, "form of life." In one place in the *Philosophical Investigations,*
Wittgenstein states, "to imagine a language means to imagine a form of
life."[11] Elsewhere he writes, "It is what human beings *say* that is true
and false, and they agree in the *language* they use. That is not agreement
in opinions but in form of life."[12] So "form of life" could refer to the fact
that human beings are linguistic; to the collection of basic agreements
out of which a particular community develops its conventions, lan-

guage, and way of life; or even to particular languages. In the latter instances, various communities could have contrasting, even contradictory forms of life that are so basic that one could not get at the roots of another community's way of dealing with the world.

Just as it is not evident that the private language arguments entail conventionalism or antirealism, similarly it is not clear that Wittgenstein meant the term "form of life" to distinguish particular, distinct, and possibly incommensurable languages or communities. Wittgenstein also writes, "The term 'language-game' is meant to bring into prominence the fact that the *speaking* of language is part of an activity, or of a form of life."[13] It may be the case, then, that language is not based on conventions or community consensus but on something more primitive. Using this starting point Merrill Hintikka and Jaakko Hintikka challenge conventionalist and antirealist interpretations of the private language arguments. Rethinking those arguments, Hintikka and Hintikka argue that the notion of a language-game, not community practice, is constitutive of human experience including language. Language-games are primitive forms of life that are the basis for all human phenomena including rule-governed activities such as language. Because language-games are by definition social activities, the idea of a private language is impossible. Contrary to Wittgenstein's alleged antirealism, Hintikka and Hintikka contend that Wittgenstein's private language arguments view "language-games as constituting the basic language-world link."[14] So this version of the private language arguments results in a species of realism and physicalism. Surprisingly, however, defending the primacy of language-games results in a kind of linguistic relativism, because alien communities could precipitate radically different language-games as the ground for their conceptual schemes such that these conceptual schemes and the resulting languages deriving from these schemes would be incommensurable with each other.

It is obvious that the original intent of the private language arguments has evolved through these fresh elucidations. Each new reading takes a point of view that carries with it a number of philosophical presuppositions and leads to differing but important conclusions. Whether or not any of these revisionary attempts are representative of what Wittgenstein was about in the *Philosophical Investigations* is probably an impossible question to answer. Nevertheless, each of these perspectives is valuable because it generates what might be considered a logical extension of Wittgenstein's arguments through consideration of what are claimed to be consistent and viable interpretations of his thought. Each continues the dialogue on the nature of privacy, each focuses on a variety of the kinds of philosophical problems the notion of a private language raises, and each is a source of solutions to related philosophical issues deriving from these arguments.

Keeping in mind what Wittgenstein set out to accomplish in his later writings, the introduction of new material on the private language arguments, and the philosophical significance of these claims, this book has three central aims. First, the private language arguments challenge an important traditional basis of philosophical analysis. Thus the first goal is to make explicit the original arguments as Wittgenstein developed them and to reiterate their implications for traditional philosophy. Second, there is a plethora of secondary literature on the private language arguments, most of which deviates substantially from the original texts. I shall analyze some of the most important reformulations of Wittgenstein's later writings that have attracted attention in the Wittgensteinian literature and that make some notable contributions to the continuing dialogue about the private language arguments and their philosophical implications.

If at least some private language arguments are valid, and I shall argue that this is the case, one needs to determine what can justifiably be derived from these arguments. So the third aim of the book is to defend a viable formulation of the private language arguments and to extend the analysis of the private language arguments to what I find to be a coherent set of conclusions concerning some perennial philosophical problems.

There are a number of difficulties with discussing and interpreting theses from the *Philosophical Investigations*. Wittgenstein is deliberately vague, points are often ambiguously made, and statements are not always carefully argued. Thus what Wittgenstein "really meant" is often obscure or controversial. Concentrating on the *Philosophical Investigations*, I shall present and defend what I take to be a viable interpretation of the later Wittgenstein. But I would by no means claim it is the only point of view. The interpretation benefits from almost forty years of literature on the *Philosophical Investigations*. A number of problems with some of the original theses have surfaced, problems not altogether anticipated in the original work. I have tried to come up with an explication of later Wittgensteinian thought that does not contradict what I take to be Wittgenstein's central arguments but which responds to some of the puzzles raised by the text. I would not presume to suggest that Wittgenstein would have argued this way or responded to his critics in this fashion. Therefore this is not a text on Wittgenstein's thought, but on

Wittgensteinian thought. It is not primarily an exposition of what Wittgenstein said or meant, but rather a more speculative bringing together of what can be derived from what I take to be a viable interpretation and logical extension of his arguments in the *Philosophical Investigations*. Because so much has been written on what Wittgenstein might have meant or intended, to extend his thinking is not without precedent or unprofitable if I can succeed in creating a coherent analysis that actually makes progress in solving some important philosophical dilemmas.

To achieve these aims, I shall begin with a restatement of various versions of what I take to be Wittgenstein's original private language arguments. I shall also examine one historical origin of the private language problem: Hume's analysis of impression in his *Treatise of Human Nature*. The original formulations of these arguments are not without their difficulties, however. I shall raise questions concerning their conclusions. In particular, two issues are of interest. Even if, as Wittgenstein carefully argues, a language cannot be formulated from private ostensive definition, this conclusion does not eliminate all possibilities for a private language, as was once thought. Moreover, that a private language is impossible does not yield the alleged conclusion that a private phenomenon makes no sense.

The second part of the book will explore in some detail the most important and influential contemporary Wittgensteinian theories that take into account a variety of definitions of a private language. These versions of the private language arguments have generated a number of philosophical conclusions that have implications for philosophy of language, philosophy of mind, and social philosophy. These conclusions are not merely an outcome of what Wittgenstein wrote or might have said but are conclusions that have become philosophical challenges in their own right. Questions concerning the status of sensations and psychological phenomena, the role of rules and rule-following, the status of truth-conditions, and the relationship between language, the community, and the world are all issues allegedly solved by the private language arguments. These solutions need to be carefully examined and in many cases questioned, not merely because they do not follow from valid private language arguments, but also because of their importance in philosophical thinking. This will be the task of Chapters 4, 5, and 6.

In these chapters I shall argue that the shortcomings of the original private arguments cannot be overcome merely by patching up the argument with a conventionalist theory. I shall challenge both a Community View of language and Kripke's skeptical reading of Wittgenstein's project. A Community View is not without textual support in the *Philosophical Investigations*, but the focus of this perspective is misdirected. Empirically it may be the case that a language "would lose its point outside a community that generally agrees in its practices,"[15] as those who hold a Community View contend. But community agreements do not form the "bedrock" or the "court of last appeal" in language formation, rule-following, or evaluation. One need not interpret Wittgenstein's notion of "form of life" this way, and such a view commits us to a consensus-based theory of language which is, I shall argue, implausible. Moreover, the antirealist conventionalism that is derived from a Community View does not follow from valid private language arguments, it does not solve the private language problems, nor is this necessarily a view defended by the later Wittgenstein.

Kripke's proposal is an interesting construal of the private language arguments. But the alleged centrality of Wittgenstein's skeptical paradox in the *Philosophical Investigations* is, at best, questionable. I shall argue that a careful reading of paragraph 201, which Kripke takes to be Wittgenstein's pivotal skeptical text, yields the conclusion that Wittgenstein solves the very questions he raises within that paragraph. Moreover, Kripke's interpretation of Wittgenstein dilutes the importance of the private language arguments as antidotes to other traditional skeptical dilemmas. Kripke's preoccupation with the role of intentions in rule-following is contrary to Wittgenstein's view of this relationship. This preoccupation erroneously places Wittgenstein in a Humean skeptical corner, the very corner that is the object of attack in much of the *Philosophical Investigations*.

Similarly, Hintikka and Hintikka's Language Game Thesis, while highlighting the central role of language games, fails as a private language argument since it cannot resolve the issue of linguistic relativism. And while it is important to show that Wittgenstein is not an antirealist, it is not patently evident that either realism or physicalism is entailed by the private language arguments.

The analysis of this variety of contemporary Wittgensteinian views, however, will not consist simply of a series of animadversions against these theories. Each position makes valuable contributions to continuing attempts at clarity in philosophy of language, and I shall derive some important philosophical conclusions from each position. Specifically, I shall conclude that the private language arguments need not imply forms of antirealism, linguistic relativism, linguistic idealism, rule-skepticism, or conventionalism. Indeed, if one takes the notion of a rule to be the "bedrock" of human activities as I shall argue in detail, problems of linguistic relativism and rule-skepticism do not arise. As a result many forms of conventionalism are brought into question, and one may begin to clear up the fuzzy notion of "form of life."

Rather than appealing to the notion of a language-game in attacking Community Views, Wittgenstein's alleged antirealism, or Kripke's skeptical rendering of the *Philosophical Investigations*, in the last part of the book I shall suggest that the private language arguments are of particular interest because of their attention to rules and rule-following. I shall strenuously argue that the notion of a rule lies at the foundation of any language, and it is this notion, rather than those of brute agreements or community practices, that is crucial in the private language arguments. While language-games play a central role in rule-following activities and the regulative function of rules, the notion of a rule, as distinct from rule-following, is constitutive of language-games as well. When Wittgenstein declares that "a great deal of stage-setting in a language is presupposed if the mere act of naming is to make sense,"[16] he is arguing that the notion of a rule, not that of ostensive definition, is the ground for language and language formulation. Thus even primitive sound-sensation associations depend on the stage-setting of simple referential rules in order to be associations at all. The idea of a rule is intrinsically connected with the concepts of "same" and "difference," so that no rule could be private in the sense that a rule could be logically unintelligible to persons other than the user of that rule. Because of the interconnections between rules, language, and language formation, the idea of a private language is an absurdity.

The book will conclude with an exploration of some of the concepts and problems relating to the admissibility of private phenomena. As a number of philosophers now recognize, the private language arguments are not arguments in support of some versions of logical behaviorism, as was once thought in some quarters. I shall carry this point further. It is not merely the case that the concept of a private mental phenomenon is not inconsistent with the belief in the impossibility of a logically private language. It is consistent with these arguments that, in principle, one can understand the words of another without access to the referents of those words. We sometimes think of sensations, feelings, and psychological phenomena as, in principle, epistemically private phenomena. I shall argue that such a radical position needs modification. However, such modifications clarify the notion of epistemic privacy and do not imply the counterintuitive conclusion that such phenomena are either merely forms of behavior or are in every sense publicly accessible to others. In contrast to some versions of a Community View, I shall defend the so-called independence thesis, the thesis that "it is logically possible that however similar two persons are in behaviour and physical construction, still their sensations or the felt quality of their experience may yet be radically different."[17] I shall argue in a positive way that indeed one can refer to phenomena that are in many important senses private and even unique, with words whose meanings are clearly understood by others.

This book, then, takes some of Wittgenstein's best-known statements and arguments in the *Philosophical Investigations* and reorganizes them into a coherent set of theses. It extends and continues a dialogue about the nature of language, communication, and privacy. This is of value, because a philosopher's lasting contribution is not merely derived from what he or she wrote or might have intended, but rather how that original set of writings continues to generate new philosophical ideas and sparks creative resolutions to philosophical puzzles. Whether Wittgenstein would have reached these conclusions is a question I shall leave to the history of philosophy, but that his works continue to generate fresh ideas and reflections I have no doubt.

Notes

1. Ludwig Wittgenstein, *Philosophical Investigations* (hereafter abbreviated as *PI*), trans. G. E. M. Anscombe (New York: The Macmillan Company, 1953), §243.
2. See, for example, Suzanne Langer, *Philosophy in a New Key* (New York: New American Library, 1948; 1962), especially Chapter 5, for a discussion of this evidence.
3. David Hume, *A Treatise of Human Nature*, ed. L. A. Selby-Bigge (Oxford: Clarendon Press, 1888), Book I, Part I, Sec. 1, p. 1.
4. See R. M. Dancy, "Alien Concepts," *Synthese* 56 (1983): 283–300, for a discussion of this problem. Dancy seems to imply that "the idea of concepts essentially different from our own" makes sense but also that, in principle at least, we can comprehend these concepts. See also Donald Davidson, "On the Very Idea of a Conceptual Scheme," *Proceedings and Addresses of the American Philosophical Association* 47 (1973): 5–20.
5. G. E. M. Anscombe, "The Question of Linguistic Idealism," *Essays on Wittgenstein in Honour of G. H. von Wright*, Acta Philosophica Fennica, Vol. 28, ed. Jaakko Hintikka (Amsterdam: North Holland Publishing Co., 1976), p. 188.
6. See Dancy, "Alien Concepts," pp. 283–285, and Anscombe, "Linguistic Idealism," pp. 188–215. See also Wittgenstein, *PI*, Part II, p. 230.

7. Christopher Peacocke, Reply [to Gordon Baker, "Following Wittgenstein: Some Signposts for *Philosophical Investigations* 143–242,"]: Rule Following: The Nature of Wittgenstein's Arguments," in *Wittgenstein: To Follow a Rule*, ed. Steven H. Holtzman and Christopher M. Leich (London: Routledge & Kegan Paul, 1981), p. 73.
8. Jack Temkin, "A Private Language Argument," *Southern Journal of Philosophy* 24 (1986): 111.
9. See Crispin Wright, *Wittgenstein on the Foundations of Mathematics* (Cambridge: Harvard University Press, 1980), p. 216.
10. Wittgenstein, *PI*, §201. See also Saul Kripke, *Wittgenstein on Rules and Private Language* (Cambridge: Harvard University Press, 1983), p. 7.
11. Wittgenstein, *PI*, §19.
12. Wittgenstein, *PI*, §241. The text says "form of life," not forms of life.
13. Wittgenstein, *PI*, §23.
14. Merrill Hintikka and Jaakko Hintikka, *Investigating Wittgenstein* (Oxford: Basil Blackwell, 1986), p. 212. Capitalized in the original text.
15. Kripke, *Wittgenstein on Rules and Private Language*, p. 96.
16. Wittgenstein, *PI*, §257.
17. Simon Blackburn, "How to Refer to Private Experience," *Proceedings of the Aristotelian Society* 75 (1974–75): 201–2.

1

"So Another Person Cannot Understand the Language"

Some of what has been written about the Wittgensteinian private language arguments, arguments purporting to show that a private language is impossible, has confusingly represented what is meant by the notion of a private language. For this reason the import of the claim that a private language is impossible varies according to one's definition of privacy and the kinds of private language arguments one derives from that definition. At the same time it is on the basis of the claim that a private language is impossible that many recent philosophers have come up with what they find to be new solutions to a number of philosophical puzzles. These include resolution of questions of relativism, conventionalism, and realism, clarity concerning the nature of so-called private "mental" experiences, and definitive understanding of the relationship of language to society and to the world. Therefore, how one defines privacy and how one lays out the private language arguments have significance for other central philosophical concerns. To evaluate the variety of private language arguments and their affect on these concerns it is essential that one first get as clear as possible about what is meant by "private language." In what follows we will see that there are three sources of possible privacy entailed in the various private language arguments: privacy of reference, privacy of rules or syntax, and/or physical or linguistic isolation of the speaker. Given these three types of privacy it will turn out that there are at least five possibilities for a so-called private language, each of which opens up different philosophical implications.

I

Let us begin with a review of Wittgenstein's statements about private language. As we saw in the Introduction, in §243 of the *Philosophical Investigations* Wittgenstein defines a private language as having the following characteristics:

> The individual words of this language are to refer to what can only be known to the person speaking; to his immediate private sensations. So another person cannot understand the language.[1]

In a later passage, §256, Wittgenstein adds a further clarification. A private language is "the language which describes my inner experiences and which only I myself can understand."[2] What Wittgenstein means, as I interpret these passages, is that there are two stipulations for a private language, (1) While I can understand my private language, it cannot be understood by another. (2a) Such a language describes my inner experiences, so that (2b) words in this hypothetical language refer to phenomena known only to the speaker, e.g., (2c) to her private sensations. Let us call such a language PL_a. What is at issue here is a logically private language, and what is meant by a non-private language is any language capable in principle of being understood by more than one person. This stipulation is a necessary condition for a private language, and whether or not the language is in fact understood by more than one person has no bearing. We shall talk more about this stipulation later in the chapter when we discuss whether or not stipulation (1) is also a sufficient condition for a private language.

Is stipulation (1) according to my scheme not part of the characterization of a private language but a condition that follows from (2)? Wittgenstein could be arguing that

> (a) the words of the [private] language are to refer to what can only be known to the speaker, (b) the words of the language are to refer to the speaker's immediate private sensations; [therefore], (c) another person cannot understand the language.[3]

This depiction of a private language, however, ignores §256, where Wittgenstein specifies that a private language is "the language which describes my inner experiences *and which only I myself can understand*" (my italics), a statement which implies that one of the characteristics of a private language is its incomprehensibility to others. It also appears to commit Wittgenstein to the position that all those languages and only those languages whose words refer to immediate private sensations and/or to phenomena knowable only to the speaker are private languages. This would eliminate the consideration of another interesting possible kind of private language, one whose rules and grammar are understood only by the speaker but whose subject matter might be publicly accessible phenomena.[4] We shall talk more about the possibility of such a language later in the chapter.

Wittgenstein stipulates that the subject matter of a private language must be "what can only be known to the speaker," which he specifies as one's inner experiences and, more specifically, one's "immediate private sensations." This stipulation does not commit one to the view that the only functions of languages are naming and describing. Nor does it commit one to the view that there are, in fact, necessarily private sensations or experiences or that if there are, these are knowable only to the speaker-experiencer. Finally, it does not imply that, since a private language must refer to private objects, a non-private language cannot so refer. The essential point is merely that one stipulation for a *private* language, according to Wittgenstein, is that it refers to objects, phenomena, or experiences that are perceivable and/or known only to one person. Since sensations are commonly thought of as private in one or both of these ways, a view Wittgenstein appears to question later in the *Philosophical Investigations*, and since one's sensation language is sometimes thought to be in a private language, Wittgenstein uses sensations as possible subject matter for a private language.

Does Wittgenstein mean in this passage that the only possible subject matter for a private language is one's immediate private sensations? Some interpreters argue that a private language is one whose subject matter could be any phenomena so long as those phenomena are known only to the speaker.[5] According to this view one's immediate private sensations are merely examples of such phenomena, and not such good ones.[6] While Wittgenstein might argue that any so-called private phenomena would be candidates as subject matter for a private language, it is clear that he deliberately chose sensations. Wittgenstein is not merely concerned to clear up how it is we think of language. He wants to question some classical approaches to philosophy that attempt to begin their philosophical analysis from what appears to be immediately given and indubitable, for example, sensations. By undermining the indubitability of such a starting point, Wittgenstein also invites us to rethink what we mean by the notion of a private object, a sensation, a private phenomenon, or a private mental phenomenon, and to do that one needs to determine what the status is of talk about such phenomena.

II

Despite Wittgenstein's preoccupation with sensation language as a possible private language, there are other possible kinds of private languages. Whether or not Wittgenstein meant to include these possibilities in his discussion of a private language, these possibilities are important both because they are widely discussed in the literature on private languages and because they take into account questions raised by the original Wittgensteinian definition of a private language. Let us look at some of them.

At least one definition of "private language" excludes the stipulation that the subject matter for a private language must be one's private sensations. One could generalize the notion of a private language as follows:

> Take any classical metaphysical problem on which there is such a thing as a Sceptical View. Now take the range of statements of which it is the relevant Sceptical View that we can never know whether or not any statement in that range is true. And now *if* the sceptic's view were correct, then what we might call the relevant term or kind of term or form of term, will be such that if a man uses that term or kind of term or form of term, he speaks a (at least partly) private language.[7]

Let us assume a sceptical view about the existence of material objects. Any statement about material objects would then necessarily belong to a private language, and one could never verify whether the word *table*, for example, stands for anything objective under these conditions.

> All that is needed for turning a class of sentences "S" into sentences of a private language is that whatever it is which is a way of finding out whether or not sentences of kind S are true should be made logically irrelevant to the truth of sentences of kind S. *Instantly* it is not possible that we should know whether or not any sentences of kind S are true; and *instantly* if a man uses sentences of kind S it is not possible that we should know what he means by them.[8]

However, the question raised by the idea of a private language is whether one can construct a language that necessarily cannot be *understood* by others, not whether the statements in that language can possibly be true. In considering any skeptical argument, for instance, the argument about the existence of material objects, one must be able to understand what the skeptic means by the term "material object." Otherwise, one could not understand what was meant by the claim that no material object statement can be verified. In general, the notion of a private language does not depend on the impossibility of verifying the truth of statements of the language, but rather on the impossibility of understanding them if the language is not one's own. To use an example, Egyptian hieroglyphics have been, for the most part, translated; that is, one understands statements made in this language. But the possibility of verifying the truth or falsity of many of the material object statements in this language is obviously impossible.

What is interesting about this proposal as a proposal for a private language is not whether we can verify the truth of material object statements. Rather, it is the implied suggestion that the meanings of terms I use to talk about material objects could be understandable only to me, since according to the skeptical view, there is no way of knowing whether my use of the term "material object" is what others mean by that expression. A second possibility for a private language, then, would be a language that (1) is understood only by its speaker and (2) whose subject matter is experienced, known, and/or knowable only to its speaker. Whether Wittgenstein would accept this particular formulation is of historical interest, but a negative answer to the historical question does not mitigate the importance of considering this sort of private language as a possibility. Let us call such a language PL_b. The difference between PL_a and PL_b is that the subject matter for PL_a is restricted to one's sensations.[9]

This discussion also suggests a third type of private language, one in which the only stipulation is that it is comprehensive in principle to only one person, its creator-speaker. Words in such a language could refer to phenomena perceivable or known to anyone. But the meanings the language attaches to such phenomena and its grammar, rules, and syntax would be such that only its speaker could understand it. Let us call such a language PL_c.

Does it make sense to speak of a private language, PL_c, the only condition for which is that it is logically incomprehensible to persons other than the language user? Let us suppose that a person, P, tries to construct such a language. Obviously, if P is to develop a private language which is understood only by herself it will not suffice for her to observe the word behavior of others and appropriately translate these words into her own language. For if P merely substitutes for the word "table" another word such as "ugug," the difference between her language and English is the same as the superficial difference between English and French, for example, and P's language is not incomprehensible to others. There is a problem in trying to imagine a language that is comprehensible only to its speaker when such a language includes the use of, or reference to, non-private objects or phenomena. For if one associates a word in any way with public phenomena, or if words in the proposed private language refer to non-private objects, this appears to allow the language to be translated by others. This is because, in both instances, one's patterns of naming could, at least in principle, be observed by others. These patterns give one a clue, a beginning with which to interpret the supposedly private language.

In the preceding paragraph we have assumed that in trying to construct or imagine a private language whose only distinguishing feature is that it is incomprehensible to anyone but P, P has at hand, and will employ, certain "logical signs" or rules such as the notions of "identity," "correctness," "same," "difference," and so on, and that these rules will be used in P's proposed language just as they are used in other non-private languages. For instance, we have assumed that when P observes a new object or event, she will try to relate it to memories of past observations of phenomena that she thinks are like the present one and compare it to memories which do not seem to be like the present phenomenon. We have assumed that P will relate repeated behavior by applying the same sounds to similar events. What makes P's language understandable is that one can observe P's patterns of naming which follow the same kinds of rules as naming, say, in English.

Following this line of argument, unless private events or phenomena knowable only to the speaker are the sole subject matter for a language, it appears that any language P constructs or speaks is comprehensible to persons other than its speaker or inventor. This is not to claim that if necessarily private experiences are the sole subject matter for a language, such a language is incomprehensible in principle to persons other than the language user. Nor are we saying that for a language to be private it must be apprehended (heard) only by P, the inventor of the language. It is just that in this case it would appear that the only chance for P's language to be private is that its subject matter is private phenomena.

However, the foregoing arguments make the rash assumption that the language P constructs will follow rules—the same kinds of rules that other familiar ordinary languages follow. But suppose P was clever enough to construct her own language rules so that when she uses the word "ugug," for example, sometimes it refers to pain and other times it functions as the verb "to go." Suppose, furthermore, that P could construct all the "rules" of her language in such a way that words which sounded the same and were spelled identically had a multiplicity of changing functions so that it was impossible to understand the rule being applied on any occasion and thus to translate P's language. If such a language could be constructed, it would qualify for a private language, PL_c, even though it referred or could refer to publicly observable phenomena. Thus PL_c is a candidate for a private language.

There are, then, at least three possibilities for a private language: PL_a in which two conditions hold: (1) that it is comprehensible only to its speaker in the sense that only the speaker can understand the language even when the language is heard by other persons, and (2b) that its subject matter must be one's private sensations; PL_b, a language in which condition (1) and condition (2a), that the subject matter must be knowable only to the speaker, hold; and PL_c, a language in which the only first condition (1) holds.

III

Are PL_a, PL_b, and PL_c the only possibilities for a private language, or is it possible to imagine a philosophically interesting private language where another condition holds true?

> [w]hat philosophers usually seem to have in mind when they speak of a private language is one that is, in their view, necessarily private, in as much as it is used by some particular person to refer only to his own private experiences.[10]

As we shall see, some of these philosophers also claim that it follows from the fact that the subject matter of a language or part of a language is private, that this language or a part of this language is logically incomprehensible to others. Let us call such a language, whose only stipulation is that its subject matter is the speaker's own private experiences, PL_d.

This sort of language, PL_d, is of great interest to the project of this book, for one of the purposes of this essay is to show how just such a language is possible. We hope to demonstrate how it is that a person, S, can refer to his own private sensations and feelings, with words that can be understood by T and others. If it can be successfully argued, as we shall try to do in subsequent chapters, that one talks about and refers to private phenomena in non-private languages, then PL_d does not differ from any ordinary language *as a language*. Unless it can be shown that if one can refer to a private phenomenon the language one uses in so referring is not comprehensible to others, or the part of it that is used to talk about sensations, for example, is not comprehensible, then a language that *is* understood by persons other than its speaker and whose only distinguishing characteristic is that it refers solely to events that are not perceivable to others, is not a private language. This is because there is nothing to distinguish this language from other, ordinary languages except its restricted subject matter. In English, for example, there are groups of words or phrases that follow the rules of the language, which are understood by most speakers of English and which apparently refer to feelings such as pains which may be private. Hence it may be the case that a language is interesting as a private language only in so far as parts of English that refer to and denote private phenomena are also interesting.

However, much work needs to be done before we can conclude that PL_d is not a private language and, conversely, that non-private languages are not problematic when referring to private sensations. It must be argued successfully both that non-private languages can refer to private phenomena and that no language or part of a language referring to private phenomena is or can be a private language.

There are other kinds of applications for the term "private language" that have been excluded by our definitions of a private language, because this definition includes the stipulation that a private language must be incomprehensible to everyone but its speaker. It could be that

> what makes a language private is simply the *fact* that it satisfies the purpose of being intelligible only to a single person or to a restricted set of people . . . The fact that only one person, or only a few people, are able to understand it is purely *contingent*.[11]

Contingently private languages such as secret codes or dead languages, languages that could, at least in principle, be understood by more than one person, should one uncover the key to translate them, differ from other, ordinary languages such as English only by the *fact* that they have not been translated. Because it is always possible at least in theory that these languages will be translated, although no living person may now understand them, these languages are not incomprehensible in principle. Hence, while secret languages are often referred to as "private languages," and while they are of interest to a linguist, they are not necessarily significant philosophically as private languages.

Contingently private languages are of interest for another reason, however. Their possibility raises the question about a fifth kind of private language, let us call it PL_e, a language that might develop outside a community, such as a language Robinson Crusoe, for example, might create. Concerning the importance of this sort of language, it has been argued that even if the private language arguments do not show that a private language is in principle logically impossible, at least these arguments "arrive at the factual conclusion that a necessarily private language is contingently impossible."[12] This is based on the observation that in fact human beings are not "linguistic self-starters"[13] but need social contact with other persons in order to develop a language. So a language such as PL_e is in fact impossible.

This sort of analysis of a private language such as PL_e raises a number of complex issues. The questions, simply put, are as follows. Does language follow rules, the existence and following of which entail (a) agreements between language users and (b) community practices or customs such that a person in isolation from these practices could not speak a language or develop one? When Wittgenstein says, "It is not possible that there should have been only one occasion on which someone obeyed a rule,"[14] does he mean that using language rules entails social practices such that (1) *in fact* one cannot use a rule in isolation by herself? Or, (2) are community practices *necessary* for a language to develop so that a fellow such as Crusoe, if physically isolated on a desert island, could not in principle create a language?[15] Or, (3) is it rather that the notion of a practice is more formal so that a rule sets a formal normative standard allowing for the repeatability of application on a number of occasions in different kinds of situations?

A number of philosophers contend that rules and rule-following are social practices. Crusoe could not produce a language in isolation without a community and community consensus. Others more cautiously claim that if someone, say Susan Crusoe, was *linguistically* isolated from a community of language users, any language development would be impossible. Without a community with which to interact and develop agreements on the uses of words Susan has not, nor can she develop, a language. I shall argue that rule-following and language use are activities, that is, practices, but they do not necessarily entail *social* practices.[16] From this perspective Robinson Crusoe could, at least in principle, develop a language in physical isolation. Such a language would employ norms or rules which, if we should come in contact with him, we could understand. So Robinson's physical isolation from other language users may or may not be a barrier to his language development. Susan's case is more complex, but, as I shall argue in Chapter 7, under certain specified conditions Susan, too, could develop a language.

There are more complications. In brief, if language is practice-bound, is language use merely conventional such that what the community or the majority views as correct usage *is* correct? Or is it the case that language rules entail normative elements by which language users can *evaluate* their own and community practices?[17] The view one adopts has consequences not only for one's view of language but also for one's views about truth-statements about the world. For if one holds a so-called Community View[18] about language development and rule-following, then it is sometimes concluded that what allegedly is a true (or false) statement is merely what the community consensus takes to be true or false, or that truth-conditions for statements turn into assertability conditions about what a community basically agrees upon. These issues, all of which will be explored more fully, arise out of a discussion of PL_e. More will be said about PL_e in Chapters 4 and 5.

IV

We have before us, then, five types of allegedly private languages, each of which plays a substantial role in some versions of the private language arguments. To summarize, they are:

PL_a: (1) comprehensible only to its speaker, and
(2) its subject matter, that is, its referring words, are only immediate private sensations, sensations that can be known only to the speaker.

PL_b: (1) comprehensible only to its speaker, and
(2) its subject matter is phenomena that can be known only to the speaker.

PL_c: comprehensible only to its speaker.

PL_d: its subject matter is immediate private sensations.

PL_e: develops in physical or linguistic isolation from social practices of a community either in fact or in principle.

Excluding secret languages from our list of private languages, that is, languages that could be understood if they were translated, heard, or read, there are at least three sources of alleged privacy to be distinguished in these various types of private languages. These include: P_1, the subject matter of the language; P_2, the structure of the language (e.g., its rules); and/or P_3, its physical or linguistic isolation from social practices.[19]

Given these possible sources of privacy, there are at least four kinds of arguments purporting to show that a private language is impossible, in one or more of the ways we have defined it. The first concerns itself with the subject matter of a private language. These arguments attempt to show that the notion of a private language is an absurdity because private experiences, the alleged subject matter of such a language, are not the proper sorts of phenomena from which one can construct or learn a language. It is with these kinds of arguments that we shall concern ourselves in Chapter 3 by reexamining the first formulations of the private language arguments and the kinds of conclusions that were drawn from them.

Second, some philosophers argue that rules and rule-following depend on consensus or agreement between persons, so that a language can develop only in a community. These sorts of arguments, which depend upon what we shall call a Community View of language, will be the topic for Chapters 4 and 5. A third kind of argument, one we shall analyze in Chapter 6, focuses attention on the notion of a language-game and argues that language-games, which cannot be private, are the basis for language, and thus no language can be private. A fourth argument concludes that the nature of a rule, rule-following, and the role of rules in the development or learning of a language are such that a private language is impossible. These arguments will be the topic for Chapter 7.

Private language arguments commonly employ at least three approaches. Some arguments focus on language construction and attempt to show that one cannot construct a private language or that any language one does construct is not a private language. Other arguments begin with the facts that (1) we speak a non-private language and (2) we commonly refer to experiences that seem to be private through a language whose words we all understand. Given these facts, one then investigates whether a private language makes sense, if so under what circumstances, and, if not, what the circumstances are that preclude such a language. A third sort of analysis pays attention to language development and purports that a language cannot develop outside certain sorts of contexts or unless certain conditions prevail. In the next six chapters we shall find all three approaches at work.

What follows will not be merely an exercise in the taxonomy of privacy and private language arguments. Nor will we focus merely on Wittgenstein's original private language arguments or on what Wittgenstein concluded or might have concluded, although these will be important considerations. The literature has elaborated on these original arguments, and philosophical dialogue has progressed beyond his initiating analysis. As we trace each kind of argument, we will also point to and evaluate the kinds of philosophical implications that are derived from each definition of a private language and the kind of argument that is defended. So it will turn out that the most acceptable private language arguments are those that are not only internally consistent but which also do not commit its proponents to other questionable or counterintuitive philosophical conclusions.

Notes

1. Wittgenstein, *PI*, §243.
2. Wittgenstein, *PI*, §256.
3. P. M. S. Hacker, *Insight and Illusion: Themes in the Philosophy of Wittgenstein* (London: Oxford University Press, 1972), p. 222.
4. Whether or not Wittgenstein is committed to considering only private languages whose subject matter is private phenomena, we shall consider this kind of private language later in the chapter.
5. Hacker may hold this view, but he does not develop it. See *Insight and Illusion*, pp. 222ff.
6. If, following Anthony Kenny and P. M. S. Hacker, one has neither infallible knowledge nor inalienable ownership of one's sensations, then sensations do not qualify as subject matter for a private language according to Wittgenstein's definition. Of course, the issue is more complicated, as we shall see. See Anthony Kenny, *Wittgenstein* (Cambridge: Harvard University Press, 1972), pp. 185–190, and Hacker, *Insight and Illusion*, pp. 248–250.
7. Judith Jarvis Thomson, "Private Languages," *American Philosophical Quarterly* 1 (1964): 29–30.
8. Ibid., p. 30.
9. Whether or not sensations *are* private phenomena will be discussed at length in a later chapter. Here we shall assume for the sake of argument that they are.
10. A. J. Ayer, "Can There Be a Private Language?" *Proceedings of the Aristotelian Society* (Suppl.) 27 (1954), reprinted in A. J. Ayer, *The Concept of a Person* (London: Macmillan & Co., 1963), p. 37.
11. Ayer, "Can There Be a Private Language?" pp. 36–37, my italics.
12. Robert J. Fogelin, *Wittgenstein* (London: Routledge & Kegan Paul, 1976), p. 165.
13. Ibid.

14. Wittgenstein, *PI*, §199.
15. See, for example, Peacocke, "Reply: Rule Following," pp. 72–95, for a version of this view.
16. This may be the view of Gordon Baker and P. M. S. Hacker. See their book, *Scepticism, Rules and Language* (Oxford: Basil Blackwell, 1984), particularly the Preface and the first chapter. See also Gordon Baker, "Following Wittgenstein: Some Signposts for *Philosophical Investigations* 143–242," in Holzman and Leich, pp. 31–71. Christopher Peacocke's article (see the preceding note) is in response to Baker.
17. Saul Kripke may hold this view, although he seems to waiver between this and the so-called community or majoritarian account of Peacocke and others. See his *Wittgenstein on Rules and Private Language*.
18. Christopher Leich and Steven Holtzman call this view a "majoritarian account" of language and the private language argument. This term is unworthy of the view, as I shall point out in Chapter 6, but it is important to consider it as an alternative to analyzing the private language argument. See Christopher Leich and Steven Holtzman, "Introductory Essay: Communal Agreement and Objectivity," in Holtzman and Leich, pp. 1–30.
19. For this distinction see Colin McGinn, *Wittgenstein on Meaning* (Oxford: Basil Blackwell, 1984), pp. 79ff.

2

"Nothing Is Ever Present to the Mind but Perceptions"

It might be concluded that the foregoing examples of private languages are trivial, because one has difficulty imagining a set of circumstances in which a language might develop that could meet any or all of these conditions. But if it is true that one cannot even imagine how a private language might develop, why is this notion considered so significant? How is it then that some contemporary philosophers find it important to argue that a private language is impossible? What is the historical significance of the notion of a private language in response to which arguments against the possibility of a private language were developed? To illustrate what is at issue at least from a historical perspective, let us examine an example of a traditional philosophical analysis that begins with the notion of a private experience and evolves the idea of a private language using definition PL_d. Specifically, let us consider the role of the term "impression" as David Hume employs it in his philosophy, particularly as he uses this idea in the *Treatise of Human Nature*.

It should be emphasized at the outset that this example will serve merely as a model, a "straw person," to illustrate a possible private language and to point to the kind of philosophical thinking against which the original private language arguments were formulated. The success (or failure) of this kind of thinking will be examined later in the book. One hopes that this analysis is an accurate account of Hume's thinking, but if it is not, nevertheless it serves as a good example for the problems we are trying to illustrate throughout the book. For it will turn out that three forms of skepticism can be interpreted from Hume's program in the *Treatise*, each of which exerts significant influence over philosophical analysis and, in the genesis of the private language arguments, many of which are constructed to counterattack such skeptical positions.

I

Hume begins the *Treatise* with these words: "All perceptions of the human mind resolve themselves into two distinct kinds, which I shall call *impressions* and *ideas*."[1] Impressions include "all our sensations, passions, and emotions, as they make their first appearance in the 'soul,'"[2] while ideas, according to Hume, are "the faint images of these [impressions] in thinking and reasoning."[3] Hence it is claimed that ideas are copies of, and derived solely from, impressions. "Impressions are internal and perishing existences and appear as such."[4] It would appear then that according to Hume having an impression is a private experience in the sense that impressions are perceivable to, and possessed by, only one person. Moreover, from Hume's analysis it could be said that one has what is sometimes called "privileged access" to one's own impressions, because, according to Hume, no one can ever perceive or directly apprehend the impression of another.

Furthermore, Hume claims that "nothing is ever present to the mind but perceptions . . . it follows that 'tis impossible for us so much as to conceive or form an idea of any thing specifically different from ideas and impressions."[5] The only data for what is known, then, would seem to be private experiences. Therefore, to relate this to the notion of language, it would appear that the only source for subject matter for a language is one's private impressions, and impressions provide the basis of, and the only means for, developing and using words and subsequently making philosophical analyses and inferences.

Hume's position can be summarized in more modern terms:

> As an oversimplification we can say that Hume held that the only possible objects of the human mind are impressions. Hence for a word to have a meaning it must be one which refers to an impression . . . Hence any intelligible sentence must refer only to possible impressions; for how is one to understand a word which has not been learnt ultimately by means of ostensive definition? Thus to know the meaning of a word is to know to what type of impression it is linked by ostensive definition.[6]

To repeat, because nothing exists over and above one's perceptions ("nothing is ever present to the mind but perceptions") and because these impressions are necessarily private phenomena ("Impressions are internal and perishing experiences"), according to Hume, it follows that the meanings of all words in any language spoken or developed by the perceiver are derived merely from his own "perishing" impressions. If this reading of Hume is correct, the meaning of any word in such a language is derived from ostensive definition and must be identified with its private reference to the type of impression or the idea involved therein. Here ostensive definition involves the initial identification of an impression by uttering a sound in its presence (a form of pointing). The utterance allegedly establishes a sound-impression connection that serves as the basis for reapplying the same sound to other similar or identical impressions. Thus the sound is established as a word referring to an impression or a class of impressions.

The relation of ostensive definition to the possibility of a private language will be discussed in Chapter 3. It should be seen here, however, that to follow the scheme of the *Treatise*, the term "ostensive definition" or, in this case, "private ostensive definition" (because the defining is done by one person solely on the basis of her own private experiences) applies in the first instance to the associations of sounds with *particular* impressions rather than to the associations of sounds as names of classes, or similar impressions. This is because, in Hume's analysis, "nothing is ever present to the mind but perceptions," each of which makes its appearance as an independent momentary impression. Hence the associations one makes are, in the first instance, with individual sensations as they appear before one's consciousness, according to this interpretation of Hume. Thus one begins with a particular impression and particular memories of impressions. This is the basis for Hume's later conclusion that the associations one makes between certain *kinds* of allegedly similar impressions and ideas are logically insupportable connections between similar but not identical impressions based on the unjustified belief or sentiment of what one remembers to be repeating perceptions of similar objects.[7]

It should be emphasized that the reason "impression" is in a private language is not merely because impressions are private experiences and/or because any reference to a private event must be in a private language. The reason that the word "impression" is in a private language, at least by this analysis of Hume's argument it would seem, is because in this instance momentary private experiences as they appear individually to one consciousness (i.e., impressions and ideas) provide the only subject matter for a language and, more importantly, the sole means for deriving the meanings of words. Thus, it follows from

Hume's claim, "'tis impossible for us so much as to conceive or form an idea of any thing specifically different from ideas and impressions,"[8] that the meaning of a word is identified with its private reference. In the resulting language, which is formed by a series of private ostensive definitions where the meaning of a word is identified with its reference, there is no way of verifying that the impressions to which one refers by sounds will be similar to the impressions to which another person refers with the same sound.

It follows from this reading of Hume that to begin with the notion of a particular private impression would seem to provide one no data with which to establish even that others have impressions, because one would know only from one's individual experiences. In this scheme one can (logically) never know whether what others are talking about when they use the sound "pain," for instance, are the same kinds of impressions to which one is referring with this sound. And even the belief that one's language could be understood by others, should it be demonstrated on other grounds that other persons exist, is not justifiable under these conditions. Because only the speaker has access to the references of his words, because each reference is unique, that is, no object of reference reoccurs to be spoken of again, and because even the term "impression" is in a private language, the language one speaks cannot be understood by others.

Moreover, it would appear that not only would it be impossible in principle for someone else to learn the language of the speaker in this case, but it would also be impossible for the speaker in this instance to learn the language of another person to explain or interpret the first. This is because, under the stipulations of the proposed argument as we have delineated it, all thinking, all analyses, and any language begin from the starting point of private ostensive definition where the sole subject matter is private and particular experiences. Thus if it is the case that one could take as one's starting point for a philosophical analysis an impression or a sense datum, that is, a phenomenon that is necessarily private and momentary in existence, and if one's only material for further philosophical inferences is these perceptions as they appear individually so that the meaning of a word is identified with its particular reference, then any language one derived or spoke could not in principle be comprehended by anyone other than its speaker. In other words should the conditions stipulated by Hume in the first books of the *Treatise* as we have interpreted it here prevail, only a private language would develop. Notice, too, that the so-called language one *could* develop would be merely a series of proper names, since no impression would reappear to be renamed. We shall discuss the status of such a "language" in a later chapter.

It follows from this line of argument that any philosophical inference concerning anything independent of an impression must be derived from impressions. It is on the basis of this idea that Hume attempts to make, but finds he cannot, any logically valid inferences concerning the independent and continuous existence of other minds, knowledge of the external world, or even the continuous existence of himself. To make any conclusions concerning the existence of an external world Hume must start from individual impressions and ideas. He argues, in brief, that the existence and content of a memory impression are never indubitable, because the original impression itself cannot be recalled to check the accuracy of the memory. What one calls the "external world" is an idea or series of ideas constructed out of present impressions and memory impressions, and each memory impression is, in turn, subject to doubt. Hence as Hume shows in more detail, belief in the independent and continuous existence of the external world is purely a matter of sentiment that unjustifiably connects separate memory impressions and present impressions to form such an idea. Moreover, one cannot make plausible inferences concerning the external world. This is because one is attempting to postulate the existence of something other than, and independent of, one's impressions and ideas. Such inferences are invalid because (a) they assume that what appear to be similar impressions are repeating or identical experiences, and (b) they presuppose causal connections between impressions, connections that are themselves never experienced.[9]

Moreover, according to Hume, one cannot catch an impression of the self, but merely its perceptions, and what one calls "I" is merely "a heap or collection of different perceptions."[10] The idea of the self, then, is a matter of ungrounded belief by this argument. And by the same kind of reasoning the belief in the continuous and independent existence of persons or even "bundles of impressions" other than one's own perceptions is, at best, doubtful.

Hence it would appear that Hume's philosophy is solipsistic as well as skeptical, because one cannot logically establish the existence *or* knowledge of the external world, other minds, or even the continuous existence of oneself. While human beings can scarcely fail to believe these things, according to Hume, these beliefs are based purely on habit or sentiment and have no logically valid foundation.

Hume's analysis has not gone beyond its starting point, the idea of an impression, nor can it go farther. Beginning merely with this notion one seems to be confined within the stipulations of a private language, and, if one is to follow this interpretation of the *Treatise*, Hume seems to have no "tools" with which to make valid inferences that go beyond these terms. The notion of "impression" has significance only for him, and because one has no perception of anything other than one's own impressions, one cannot infer the existence of anything that is independent of these individual impressions.

This sort of conclusion, obviously, brings into question the relation of Hume's philosophical pronouncements to the truth of his philosophy. For if what Hume claims in the first book of the *Treatise* is valid, all philosophy too must be merely a matter of sentiment. But what is important for our task in this essay is not that certain philosophical problems may or may not be solved by a certain philosophy. A program that leads to a form of solipsism is not untenable simply because one may prefer another sort of conclusion. What is meant to be seen is that this kind of philosophical methodology, when carried to its logical conclusion as Hume so carefully does and as we have interpreted it here, leads to just this sort of dead end. What is important here is that if one begins philosophical analyses from the starting point of a particular private impression and if one's inferences are made in a language developed from private ostensive associations where the meaning of a word is identified with its reference, it would appear that one cannot make valid judgments that in any way go beyond one's individual private experiences and the stipulations of one's necessarily private language. Thus the existence of anything other than one's own impressions as they appear individually to oneself cannot be established from this point of view.

Hume's idea of an impression, then, as we have depicted it, illustrates the conditions under which a private language might develop, and it points to the kinds of problems that arise out of an analysis carried out within the presuppositions of a private language. This illustration serves as a good model to point to what has traditionally been involved in the idea of a private language and to show why private language arguments evolved in the first place. For if one can show that a private language is impossible, then such an analysis fails as an *analysis* and as a model for one kind of approach to philosophical questions.

II

Whether or not the foregoing account is a correct interpretation of Hume's arguments, this example is useful for seeing how the private language arguments have affected certain traditional approaches to philosophy. If one wishes to establish as a starting point for a philosophical analysis what is immediately and indubitably given, such as an impression or a sense datum, so that one's inferences are to be drawn only from these allegedly immediate indubitable givens, one cannot go beyond this at all, in any way, not even so far as to establish words that refer to these impressions or sense data. For in order to make inferences linking individual impressions or sense data one would introduce certain concepts with which to make such inferences and thereby beg the question.

Some Humeans, however, object to such a radical interpretation of the *Treatise*. For Hume does not talk about the random primitive association of impressions and ideas but notices that the association of impressions is "guided by some universal principles"[11] of association that appear to be "qualities" of the imagination. These are, as readers are well familiar, "Resemblance, Contiguity in time and place, and Cause and Effect."[12] The status of these so-called principles is unclear, but they appear to be subjective dispositions or functions of the imagination.[13] What is interesting about them from the perspective of private languages and private language arguments is that one can make the case that Hume does not have a private language problem in the sense of trying to develop a language merely from private ostensive definitions of individual impressions. This is because it is not merely that one's *tabula rasa* receives impressions willy-nilly; it also sorts them out and links them according to those simple associative functions. The subjective principles of association, then, serve as guidelines or "rules" for organizing and reapplying sounds to impressions so that one can project patterns for the reuse of sounds onto one's disparate impressions and ideas. Thus the sounds one utters in the presence of impressions are not simply signs or primitive proper names but can have meaning as words denoting the data of one's impressions by linking similar sensations with the same name. Thus while it may be true that one cannot develop a language merely from sound-impression associations, it might be argued that Hume never thought one could.

Putting aside the problem of the status of Hume's principles of association in Hume's philosophical scheme, this reading of Hume does not let us off the skeptical hook, but it changes the form of the skeptical problem as it relates to private languages and the private language arguments. If one can develop a language from associating one's private impressions through the projective functioning of subjective qualities of the imagination onto distinct impressions and ideas, how does one know that one's own private "principles" or "rules" of association have anything to do with the rules of association others allegedly use to form their language or languages? Might it be that the language I speak merely follows my own habits and customs, which have nothing what-soever to do with your language rules and customs? In this case it is not merely that I do not know whether you and I refer to the same object when we utter the word "table," for example, that is, that the referring words of my language are the same as the referring words of the same-sounding utterances in your language. Rather, the problem is that I have no assurances that the grammar and syntax I use are similar to yours. For it could be the case that my associative principles and thus language rules are utterly different. The language I speak would be a private language according to this form of skepticism. Since there is no guarantee that language rules are similar, there is no guarantee that *any* language is not a private language.[14] Let us call this view Rule Skepticism.[15]

The challenge for the private language arguments is to show not merely that private sound-impression associations are not possible start-ing places for language. The arguments must also respond to the Rule Skeptic's challenge that one cannot know whether one's language rules are similar to another's by showing that language, language rules, and language development preclude the kind of skeptical position. And, in responding to Rule Skepticism, we must determine whether the notion of a private rule, that is, a rule that is understandable to only one person, makes sense. The challenge is not merely to show that Rule Skepticism is an absurdity, but also to show, given that language is public (that is, understandable by communities of speakers), that one could not even construct a private-rule language because of the notion of "rule." This will be the task for Chapter 7.

III

There is yet another issue arising from this analysis of Humean skep-ticism. This issue is, at best, implicit in Hume's philosophy and is certainly not stated by Hume in exactly the way many contemporary philosophers formulate the problem. Yet it arises from Hume's skepticism about the external world and other minds. The issue is as follows. Bracketing the question of whether or not language rules are or can be private (understandable only to the speaker of the language), language users have another, more serious problem. Let us consider ostensive definition. Simply put, if the so-called principles of association are merely subjective, how can I be sure I am applying the principle of resemblance, for example, the same way each time I name an impression? Do I know that the rule I am using, say, ostensive pointing, is the same as the last time I employed that rule, or thought I had employed it? In other words, how do I know privately that I am applying a rule, any rule, in the same way each time I employ it? How do my past intentions (e.g., to name objects) relate to my present ones so that I know I am applying a rule (e.g., linking sounds to objects) in a consistent way each time? Let us call this position Radical Rule Skepticism, for if it makes sense, it eliminates the possibility of the development of any language whatsoever.

Saul Kripke, in his recent book, *Wittgenstein on Rules and Private Language*, argues that this sort of skeptical issue is the central problem the *Philosophical Investigations* addresses. As Kripke puts it, "The important problem for Wittgenstein is that my present mental state does not appear to determine what I *ought* to do in the future."[16] Kripke interprets the following passage from the *Philosophical Investigations* as Wittgenstein's recognition of an unsolvable paradox surrounding the notion of a rule and rule-following: "This was our paradox: no course of action could be determined by a rule, because every course of action can be made out to accord with the rule."[17]

Kripke compares Wittgenstein's alleged skepticism about rule-following, the questioning of "the nexus between past 'intentions' or 'meanings' and present practice,"[18] with Hume's skepticism about causation and the principle of induction. Hume shows that one cannot justify the so-called laws of causation or the principle that nature is uniform except by induction from a finite number of past events occurring in conjunction with each other, the *causal* relationships of which depend on the principle one is trying to establish, to wit, the principle of the uniformity of nature. Similarly, Wittgenstein, according to Kripke, argues that one cannot guarantee the consistent content or application of a rule or use of a word from a finite number of past uses of that rule. I cannot justify my present application of a rule except by appealing to a finite number of past applications. I have no criteria independent of past and present usage with which to judge how I am to go on and whether or not I am using a rule correctly. Since we are trying to justify the consistency of our application of rules merely on the basis of past consistency of application we have no independent criterion for evaluating such a judgment. This conclusion is a radical one because, if it makes sense, it follows that words have no meaning, since there is no guarantee of consistent use. So-called rules of language are not rules since one is never sure whether or not one is reusing a rule, using a rule correctly or incorrectly or consistently, or using a new rule. So one never knows what is a correct or incorrect use of a rule or a word, and thus language is impossible.

This is obviously a more radical position than either form of Humean skepticism discussed earlier. In those more traditional skeptical views one does know whether or not one is using a rule correctly or incorrectly from a subjective point of view. It is just that the objects of reference, for example, the external world and the existence of other language users, and/or the similarity of my language rules to yours are in question.[19] In this more radical view, I do not even know whether *I* am using the word "know" correctly since I cannot judge my own "correct use" except from memories of a finite number of past uses, the correctness of which cannot be ascertained by any independent criterion.

Whether or not Wittgenstein saw this skeptical paradox as the central subject matter of the *Philosophical Investigations* is a hotly debated issue.[20] Nevertheless, even if this position is absurd, as some commentators have claimed,[21] the paradox itself is one that any study of the private language arguments must face and respond to, because Radical Rule Skepticism challenges the foundations of language, truth, and knowledge itself. In the next chapters we shall respond to this paradox as well as to the more traditional skeptical problems mentioned earlier, first by examining the importance of subject matter to an allegedly private language; second, in Chapters 4, 5, and 6, by analyzing the role of language-games, rule-following, social practices, and community agreement in language and language development; and, finally, in Chapter 7, by tackling the notion of a rule and its role in language and private languages.

Notes

1. David Hume, *A Treatise of Human Nature*, ed. L. A. Selby-Bigge (Oxford: Clarendon Press, 1888), Book I, Part I, Sec. 1, p. 1.
2. Ibid.

3. Ibid.
4. Ibid., Part IV, Sec. II, p. 194.
5. Ibid., Part II, Sec. VI, p. 67.
6. J. O. Urmson, *Philosophical Analysis* (Oxford: Clarendon Press, 1956), pp. 107–108.
7. Hume, Book I, Part II, Sec. II, pp. 251–263. See also Antony Flew, *Hume's Philosophy of Belief* (London: Routledge & Kegan Paul, 1961), pp. 18–52, which supports this interpretation of Hume.
8. Hume, Book I, Part II, Sec. IV, p. 67.
9. Ibid., Sec. VI, pp. 66–68, and Part VI, Sec. II, pp. 187–218.
10. Ibid., Part IV, Sec. II, p. 207.
11. Ibid., Part I, Section IV, p. 10.
12. Ibid., p. 11.
13. The ontological status of the faculty of imagination is also unclear.
14. See Chris Swoyer, "Private Languages and Skepticism," *Southwestern Journal of Philosophy* 7 (1977): 41–50.
15. Baker and Hacker use this term in *Skepticism, Rules and Language* to refer to the kind of skepticism Kripke attributes to Wittgenstein (pp. 60ff). I shall call that kind of skepticism "Radical Rule Skepticism" or "Rule Skepticism." See Section III of this chapter.
16. Kripke, *Wittgenstein on Rules and Private Language*, p. 56.
17. Wittgenstein, *PI*, §201.
18. Kripke, *Wittgenstein on Rules and Private Language*, p. 62.
19. See G. P. Baker and P. M. S. Hacker, "Critical Study: On Misunderstanding Wittgenstein: Kripke's Private Language Argument," *Synthese* 58 (1984): 410, on this point.
20. See, especially, Don Mannison, "Hume and Wittgenstein: Criteria versus Skepticism," *Hume Studies* 13 (1987): 138–165. Mannison argues that Wittgenstein could not have been a Humean skeptic.
21. Baker and Hacker, for instance, say this in "Critical Study."

3

"The Language Which Describes My Inner Experiences"

In ordinary language we commonly use terms such as "sensation," "pain," "dream," "image," "thought," "intention," and "belief" to refer to perceptions, sensations, feelings, activities, and phenomena that are in some sense private or not shared or shareable with other people. Sometimes dreaming, imagining, intending, thinking, and believing are called mental or psychological activities, and dreams, images, beliefs, and thought are called "mental states." The physical/mental distinction raises a number of issues peripheral to the present focus. What is important is to make sense out of this common usage, to find out what we mean by these terms, to spell out the status of their privacy, and to explain how it is we can refer to, talk about, and understand these personally peculiar activities, events, and phenomena. If the language with which one refers to and designates sensations and psychological phenomena is a private language, it is likely that the data of my sensations and psychological experiences are comprehensible only to me. But if a private language is an absurdity, one must make sense out of how it is we have dialogue about so-called private phenomena.

In this chapter we are concerned with a prior issue that is a preamble to answering questions about sensations and psychological phenomena: whether or not one can construct a language merely from one's immediate sensations. The first stage of this task is to analyze those private language arguments that focus primarily on the definition of a private language in the sense of PL_a, a language whose subject matter is the speaker's immediate sensations and which only the speaker can understand. The construction of such a language, a language formulated by private sound-sensation associations, it will turn out, is impossible. The impossibility of constructing a language merely from one's immediate sensations has alleged implications for explicating the notion of a private, mental, or psychological phenomenon. I shall examine two such theses that argue that the private language arguments establish the substantive conclusion that one cannot make sense out of a necessarily private phenomenon. Then I shall defend the counterclaim that the alleged questionability of the notion of a private phenomenon cannot be derived from the private language arguments.

I

Arguments refuting the possibility of a private language were formulated by Wittgenstein and others at least in part to meet the difficulties resulting from what we have called a Humean kind of philosophical analysis by attempting to bring into question the presuppositions of such a methodology. As we saw in Chapter 2, if the meanings of words could be derived solely from one's particular private experiences such as from one's individual impressions, it would appear that the resulting language would be a private language. Hence, if it can be shown that such a language cannot be so derived, then any analysis that begins with the notion of an individual private phenomenon and attempts to derive a language merely from ostensive sound-sound associations is thereby subject to question.

One formulation of the original private language argument is in the form of a *reductio ad absurdum*. Let us call this argument the Original Private Language Argument (OPLA). One tries to imagine a certain set of conditions under which a private language could be constructed, and then it is shown that the "language" that could be derived from this set of circumstances is not a language at all. Let us try to imagine a situation in which a man, Q, tries to construct a private language. If the private language is in the form of PL_a, referential words in that language must denote necessarily private objects or events, that is, things or experiences that are perceivable to, knowable by, or available to only one person, in this case, Q's own private experiences such as his sensations. Let us suppose that Q tries to construct a private language merely from his sensations. Q begins by trying to name a sensation. On its first occurence Q utters the sound, "pain." Q has two challenges: (1) He must try to reidentify correctly the same or similar sensation when it reoccurs, and (2) Q must try to correctly and consistently reapply the sound "pain" as a word. That is, when a second sensation occurs Q must be able to decide whether it is, or is not, sufficiently like the first so that he could call the second sensation "pain" too, and he must learn how to apply sounds to sensations correctly and consistently as words.

How can Q distinguish a correct memory from an incorrect one in this instance in order to decide whether he is using the word "pain" consistently? How does Q learn to apply the sound "pain" correctly and consistently as a name to present and new sensations? By Wittgenstein's initial definition of a private language as PL_a, Q cannot appeal to public objects in trying to reidentify a sensation. The only basis Q has for identifying the second sensation or checking the accuracy of his first identification is the memory of the previous sensation or memories of other sensations. But, according to proponents of this argument, Q cannot discover the difference between what *seems* to Q to be correct from what, by some standard independent of Q, *is* correct in applying the word "pain" on the basis of memories of previous sensations, because Q cannot appeal to anything apart from his impressions and memories to establish this distinction. At best, Q can only say that the second sensation "seems like" the first one.

But, it is argued, it is not merely the case that Q cannot distinguish what *seems* to be pain from what *is* a pain. Q cannot even make self-distinctions between what seems to him to be a pain from what seems to him not to be. The concepts "correct," "same," "right," "consistent," and so on are not available to Q under these conditions, because for these concepts to be used in a particular context, one must be able to imagine something that is *not* an instance of them. For example, if one cannot recognize the difference between unlike things, one could not use the concept of identity, because this concept could apply indifferently to everything. Similarly, it is argued, the notion of "correct" needs the concept of "incorrect" in order to be meaningfully employed. For example, one could not say that two sensations were the same unless one had some idea of a sensation that was different from the two to be identified. Hence Q cannot identify a particular sensation as "pain" unless he can also recognize a sensation that is different from a pain sensation. Unless Q has some idea of what it is to be wrong in applying the word "pain" to his sensations he will not be able to reidentify a sensation correctly.

To reiterate, Q seems to have two problems: (1) the difficulty of reidentifying a sensation, that is, the veracity of Q's memory, and (2) the challenge to develop the use of the sound "pain" as a meaningful word. It could be argued that Q's problem is the former one. It could be the case that Q has a language already and that Q is merely going through the exercise of trying to construct a private one. Therefore Q understands how language and thus words function, he knows how to refer, and he knows how to develop the sound "pain" into a word. Q's problem is that he cannot depend upon his memory, which is all he has to work with in this context, and therefore Q cannot verify his own reidentification of his sensations. According to this analysis of the argument, since sensations and memories alone are not the proper sorts of objects for reference, Q cannot construct a private language.[1]

Perhaps, however, Q is trying to develop a language from scratch without depending on a previously developed linguistic framework. By starting Q from a "linguistically naked" position one avoids the obvious criticism that the veracity of one's memory is not a problem peculiar to speakers of a private language and thus that Q's alleged difficulty in constructing a language begs the question.[2] In that case Q's problem is not that he cannot remember he was in pain or even that he associated the sound "pain" with a sensation. It is that Q does not understand what the sound "pain" *means*. Q may or may not correctly reidentify his sensations with the sound, but because he has no criteria independent of his sensations, he cannot (a) develop a consistent use of the term or (b) sort out "pain" from uses of other sounds and other sensations. It is not the truth or falsity of the pain-sensation association or the veracity of Q's memory that is at issue, but rather it is the failure to establish the meaning of the sound "pain" as a word which is in question.[3]

From these considerations (i.e., that Q cannot establish the sound "pain" as a word) it is argued that without some standard independent of his sensations to which Q can appeal for comparing and identifying a sensation as the same or as a different phenomenon, Q cannot justify his use of the word "pain." Although Q has memories of sensations other than pain, he cannot even distinguish what seem to be a pain sensation from what seems to Q not to be a pain, because Q cannot test the correctness or incorrectness of his memories except by still another memory. Because Q has at hand only the memories of previous sensations there is no way for Q to judge whether he is using the word "pain" consistently, since he has no means to develop even his own self-distinctions and thereby to set up his own standards for deciding which sensations are pain sensations. Thus, it is claimed, there is no reason why Q could not call any sensation "pain," for neither can he verify his uses of words by standards independent of his sensations, nor has Q any way to ascertain from his own impressions what would count as a correct or an incorrect sound-sensation association.

Beginning the construction of a language merely by trying to associate a sound or a sign with a private phenomenon provides Q with no means to make self-distinctions or criteria independent of these sensations with which to consistently reassociate the sound or sign with another sign. No word can be given meaning merely by introspecting certain private experiences. Associating signs with private phenomena is not a possible starting point for a language, because in order for the resulting sound-object associations to be meaningful, one needs to establish or appeal to standards for knowing what counts as a correct association. This is not possible for Q in this case. The language one tries to formulate under these conditions is an absurdity. Hence, it is concluded, a private language is impossible.

II

In this formulation of the private language argument, OPLA, there is some confusion as to how one should interpret the second stage of this argument. What is it that is missing in one's attempt to construct a private language from one's private experiences? What is meant by the expression, "standards independent of Q's sensations and memories"? Are these (a) reidentifiable objects to which words in a language could refer; (b) community customs for rule-following that specify correct and incorrect applications of sounds as words; (c) conventions or rules for the uses of words and expressions according to which not every possible application of the word or expression would be a correct one; or (d) language-games in which reference to a sensation is part of that game? These four interpretations of this part of the argument result, in each case, in different kinds of conclusions. If case (a) is being argued, then the claim is that private phenomena are not the proper sorts of "objects" that one can employ for reidentification and verification of one's uses of words. The resulting conclusion is that a language whose sole subject matter is necessarily private phenomena cannot develop under *any* circumstances because these "events" cannot be used as referents of words.[4] We shall call this kind of analysis the Strong Private Language Argument (SPLA). While this form of the private language argument is no longer popular in the literature, it is useful nevertheless to see how the notion of a private language and the private language arguments were originally interpreted, because this interpretation has had a strong influence on what was thought to be Wittgenstein's notion of a private experience, and thus this sort of argument has influenced the course of some discussions about philosophy of mind that derive from a Wittgensteinian point of view.

A weaker interpretation of case (a) is that while private phenomena might be referents for words, a language cannot develop *in the first instance* from particular private sensations, and hence a private language cannot be formed from this starting point. Let us call this kind of argument the Weak Private Language Argument (WPLA). In Chapters 4, 5, 6, and 7 we shall consider private language arguments that have in mind the definition of a standard as (b), (c), or (d).

Proponents of the Strong Private Language Argument contend that what is missing when one attempts to construct a language from one's own sensations are the proper sorts of referents with which one can verify one's sound-object associations. The argument, in summary, is as follows:

> . . . a private language is postulated; we call it a language because it is supposed to have words, and these are supposed to be used to refer, a linguistic activity. But, so the argument runs, because the *supposed* referents [e.g., pain sensations] of these supposed words are "private," in a certain special sense, *reference to them is in fact impossible,* and the supposed words are not words at all, from which it follows that the supposed language which they constitute or belong is no language at all.[5]

To illustrate this argument, suppose that P begins the construction of a private language merely by trying to identify and name a sensation. According to this argument, in this kind of situation P cannot correctly reidentify and name his sensations even if P has "logical signs" or rules at hand to use in such identifications. The private "object" at issue, that is, the present pain sensation, is not the sort of "thing" one can observe or examine to confirm one's identifications. To ascertain the kind and quality of a present sensation, P can merely appeal to memories of the same phenomenon or to memories of different sensations. Hence P's impression that he has identified two sensations as similar or as "pain" cannot be confirmed except by other memory impressions.

But, Wittgenstein argued, "what would *show* that your memory impression is false—or true? Another memory impression? Would this imply that memory is a court from which there is no appeal?"[6] Any memory impression could count as a "memory of a pain sensation," according to this interpretation of the private language argument, because there is no independent means to ascertain which memory impressions are correct or incorrect except by appealing to still other memories which themselves cannot be tested for correctness. Notice, again, as in the discussion of OPLA, the issue here is not whether P can or cannot remember his sensations or even make sound-signs for them. It is that he cannot develop words to refer to his sensations because in this case he has no verifiable objects other than his sensations and memories with which to compare and evaluate them.

It is concluded that private experiences do not provide the proper referents to develop a language, because one cannot establish the identity of one's sensations merely from present sensations and memory impressions. A private language is an absurdity, because in no circumstances can private experiences provide the proper referential material to verify one's uses of words and hence to establish a language.

Recalling OPLA, in connection with that argument it was said there that in attempting to construct a private language Q could distinguish neither (a) what seemed to him to be a correct identification of a sensation from what seemed to him to be incorrect, nor (b) what seemed to him correct from what *was* correct in trying to name his sensations. According to the Strong Private Language Argument, to develop a language it is not enough that P can distinguish what seems to P to be a pain, for example, from what P thinks are other sensations. In trying meaningfully to apply a sound to a sensation P must also be able to appeal to some *standard of pain* independent of what he thinks is a correct identification of his sensation in order to be certain P is making the correct identification. In other words, P must conclusively *verify* his identification so that he can distinguish what merely seems to him to be a pain sensation from what truly is a pain. It is essential not only (i) that P thinks he is correctly reidentifying phenomena he is trying to name so that (ii) P can in some way verify his identifications, but also (iii) that P conclusively verifies or makes certain that he is making correct associations. Following this kind of reasoning, the only way P could know he was using the term "pain" correctly would be to have another instance of this sensation independent of his perceptions at hand, such as pain, with which to compare the sensation in question. Since this kind of strong verification is ruled out in the case of sensations, it is concluded that these phenomena are not the proper objects for linguistic reference.[7]

III

According to some proponents of the Strong Private Language Argument it follows from this argument that, in general, the notion of a necessarily private phenomenon is unintelligible. Let us call this position the Private Phenomenon Argument, an argument that results in logical behaviorism. Let us suppose that the sensation of pain is a necessarily private experience. If someone, R, experiences a pain, and if pain is a private experience, then proponents of the Private Phenomenon Argument ask, "How, if pains are necessarily private, could [s]he [R] know what a pain is; how could [s]he have learned this?"[8] These philosophers claim that R could learn to identify her pains neither from someone else nor from her own experiences, and hence the idea of a private phenomenon cannot develop. The arguments in support of this conclusion are as follows.

If R's sensations are private, R could not have learned what pains are from others, because "a proponent of the privacy of sensations rejects circumstances and behavior as a criterion of the sensations of others."[9] Moreover, if pains are private, circumstances and behavior *cannot* be criteria for saying that R is in pain. These non-private events cannot establish the existence of nonobservable phenomena, because one cannot verify the existence of R's private sensations with these public criteria. Hence if public behavior cannot be criteria for saying that private events occur, and if no one has access to R's sensations except R, others cannot know that R is in pain. In this instance, "[S]He [R] could not have been taught by someone else to identify pains . . . for no one else could know when indeed [s]he [R] had a pain and hence tell him when it was correct to say [s]he had one."[10] According to this reasoning, if R's pains are private, she can learn what they are only from her own experiences. But it follows from the Strong Private Language Argument that it is a "mistaken assumption that one learns from one's own case what thinking, feeling, sensation are,"[11] because there are no means to learn privately what a sensation is or how to reidentify one's own sensations. Judging merely from her own experiences R has no standards by which to decide which of her sensations are pains; hence R alone could not correctly decide to which sensations to apply the word "pain."

Therefore, because one cannot learn what private experiences are or how to talk about them either from others or from one's own experiences, "the notion of a necessarily private (mental) phenomenon is unintelligible."[12] Conversely, it follows that if the notion of a private phenomenon makes sense, then, according to the Private Phenomenon Argument, one is also committed to a private language to talk about and refer to these phenomena. But since this sort of private language is ruled out by the Strong Private Language Argument, one does not have a "private language problem."

Let us look at an analysis of a specific psychological phenomenon other than pain, Norman Malcolm's explanation of dreaming. The implications of this analysis further illustrate problems with the Private Phenomenon Argument. In his book, *Dreaming*, Malcolm tries to clear up philosophical problems that surround such questions as, "How does one distinguish waking from sleeping?" and "How do you know you are not dreaming all the time?" In particular, he wants to show that sleeping is distinguished from all or any kind of conscious experience, and that dreaming, which occurs only when one is asleep, cannot be identified with any other "mental activity." Malcolm wants to bring into question what he calls the "Cartesian view of dreams." According to Malcolm, the Cartesian view argues that

> a) . . . since dreams can be remembered, they must be conscious experiences . . . It is correct to say that a dreamer is really aware of the contents of his dream . . .
> b) To say that one dreams is to say that one sees, hears, touches, etc., while asleep . . . We should maintain, with Descartes, that if anyone dreams that [s]he believes, doubts, expects, desires, etc., then [s]he really does.[13]

In attacking the Cartesian view Malcolm first argues that just as it is impossible seriously to state "I am dead" or "I am unconscious," one cannot seriously say "I am asleep." One cannot verify that one is asleep, or dead, so these present first-person expressions cannot be used as statements or judgments.

Next Malcolm argues that one cannot make judgments while asleep. The argument is as follows:

1. If a person, R, could make judgments while asleep, she should be able to judge that she is asleep.
2. But since R cannot "verify" (Malcolm's word) that she is asleep, she cannot make such a judgment, since she cannot use "I am asleep" meaningfully.
3. Therefore, R cannot make any judgment *whatsoever* while asleep. In

order to know what judgment R made, R would have to know R's words and that R was aware that she had uttered them, that is, someone would have to have been aware that R was making a judgment. But this can be established only if it is also determined that R (who made the judgment) was not asleep.

4. If R claims, "I made a judgment while dreaming," Malcolm asks, "How did she know she was dreaming while she was asleep? How was R aware of making the judgment?" The point is that R can dream R made a judgment, but this is dreaming, not making a judgment.

Malcolm says that such an argument can hold, *mutatis mutandis*, for all "activities" that philosophers and psychologists claim occur while one is asleep, except for dreaming, for there are no means of verifying that these activities happen, that is, according to Malcolm, there is no criterion for saying that any of these events occurred while one was asleep. The conclusion is that one does not see, hear, judge, and so on while asleep, although Malcolm does not deny point blank that one can dream that one is seeing or judging.

It might be objected that the latter is all that the Cartesians are concluding. But I think Malcolm's argument is that the Cartesians (at least the Cartesians he has in mind) hold that various activities actually occur while one is sleeping and dreaming, and Malcolm is arguing that they do not occur; one merely dreams that they occur. The thrust of Malcolm's argument is to lead up to the conclusion that there is only one activity that can occur while one is asleep (dreaming) and that this experience cannot be identified with any other conscious or psychological activity, since these activities cannot occur during sleep.

Malcolm points out that, excluding daydreams, one cannot dream unless one is asleep. Therefore, it is impossible truthfully to say "I am dreaming," just as it is impossible truthfully to say "I am asleep." However, unlike other activities that one might claim occur while one is asleep, one can verify that one has dreamed. This is because "[h]is waking impression is what establishes that he had a dream, and his account of his dream establishes what the content of his dream was."[14]

One's waking impressions are the origin of the concept of "dream," then, and it is from these impressions and reports that one learns what one has dreamed and that others have had dreams. Therefore, the criterion or basis for saying "I had a dream" is one's waking impression. When one asks, "How do you know that R dreamed?" the answer is that R told about the dream when she woke up. Thus the criterion for saying that someone else dreamed is that person's report of his dream. Furthermore, dream reports and one's impressions of one's own dreams are the *only* criteria for saying that one dreamed, according to Malcolm. Malcolm's intent, I believe, is to bring into question the Cartesian use of experiences such as dreams as phenomena to which one has epistemic and ontological privileged access, but in that attempt he perhaps exaggerates the verifiability criterion for dreaming.

Interestingly, Malcolm dismisses some psychologists' criteria for dreams (e.g., eye blinking, brain waves, etc.) as not being criteria at all for dreaming. Malcolm defines a "criterion" as "something that settles a question with certainty."[15] The reason he rejects criteria other than reports and impressions as criteria for dreams is that the concept of "dream" is obtained not from dreams, which themselves are not observable because they occur during one's sleep, but from impressions and reports, that is, from the first-person and third-person criteria for saying of someone that she dreamed. Hence if a criterion settles a question of dreaming with certainty, and if eye blinking, for example, were a criterion of dreaming, Malcolm argues that we would have a different concept of dreaming. However, while dream reports are a basis for saying that R dreamed, one would not want to deny the possible validity of psychologists' criteria as Malcolm does, where such criteria have been established by very probable evidence such as one-to-one correlations between eye blinking, for example, and remembered dreams.

It is obvious that a dream is not an impression or a report, but it is that of which one has had an impression or made a report. But Malcolm says that dreams are not logically independent of dream impressions and reports. Moreover, he claims that

> If we try to suppose that mankind might have told dreams without ever having dreams, or might have had dreams without ever having told dreams, we are in an embarrassment as to what would establish the existence of a dream.[16]

Therefore, according to this quotation, the meaning of the word "dream" (the concept of "dream") is not independent of the criteria for saying that one dreamed, although Malcolm does go quite so far as to say that they are identical.

About dreams themselves Malcolm says,

> If we cease to ask *why* it is that sometimes when people wake up they relate stories in the past tense under the influence of an impression, then we see dream-telling as it is—a remarkable human phenomenon,

a part of the natural history of man, something *given*, the foundation for the concept of dreaming.[17]

Dream-telling, then, using Wittgensteinian terms, is a "form of life," beyond which one should cease to wonder about the cause of and the reasons for dream-telling, according to this analysis.

IV

It is clear that if one accepts the Strong Private Language Argument, the foundations of an analysis such as Hume's, interpreted as we have in Chapter 2, are brought into question. According to the SPLA one cannot begin doing philosophy merely from the starting point of a particular private experience such as an impression, because from that point of view one cannot even derive a language with which to make further philosophical inferences.

There are, however, difficulties with the Strong Private Language Argument and thus with the Private Phenomenon Argument. First, is one, or must one be, always certain about one's use of words? Must every use of a denoting word be verifiable or verifiable by another instance of the object denoted? Can one formulate a language (i) when one can distinguish what seems to be a correct identification of a sensation from what seems not to be, and/or (ii) when one can sufficiently verify one's identifications for the satisfaction of one's own criteria of identification? Or can it be said that a language can develop only (iii) when one can say with certainty "I am in pain," that is, when one can appeal to some standard or object independent of what one thinks are correct identifications to verify with certainty one's use of words?

Consider again that P tries to construct a language from his sensations, and let us grant for the sake of the argument that P has at hand or is able to employ at least some simple rules for identification and naming. This assumption should not bias the outcome, because the availability of rules is not precluded by the SPLA. When a sensation occurs that seems to P to be like others he has had, P decides to refer to resembling sensations with the same sound (e.g., "pain"). In this case if P decides to refer to what seem to be similar sensations with the same sound, or if in doing so P thinks he is distinguishing his sensations in some way, then P is at least implicitly employing some patterns or conventions for using words. For having thought to refer to similar sensations, P must have some idea of what sensations are not similar to the ones he has called "pain." Hence P must have some idea of the notions of "sameness" and "difference," for example, that he can employ in applying the word "pain" to different sensations. Under these circumstances P cannot verify that what he calls "pain" in this case is like whatever he earlier called "pain" either by comparing the present sensation to another identical sensation or by appealing to pain descriptions of others. But given that P understands the concepts that we signify by such words as "correct," "same," and so on and knows how to apply them, P could compare present simultaneously occurring sensations such as a headache to a pain in P's arm. Moreover, P could compare present sensations to memories of other sensations through the notions of identity and difference, and these notions could establish the correctness or incorrectness of P's memory impressions on a comparative basis with each other. P can even set aside some memories of pain sensations as "criteria" to measure and compare other pains, when they occur, and other sensations. Even if P cannot appeal to pains other than his to be sure that he is correctly identifying his sensations, P can establish "think-criteria" from his memory impressions by which he can distinguish what he thinks are pains from what he thinks are different phenomena. Even if P's identifications are not verified or verifiable in the sense that they are certified by objects independent of P, nevertheless P's identifications may be satisfactorily verifiable to P by his own standards.

In this way P could at least establish consistently replicable word-sensation associations with which he could reidentify and name his sensations and correct his mistakes, although by some public definition other than P's own, P might be wrong.[18] If P has some idea of what it is to apply a word correctly or incorrectly, P can set up his own "standards" for verifying uses of words without appealing to publicly observable phenomena to establish the meaning of a word referring to a private experience. Hence it would appear that, counter to the claims of the Strong Private Language Argument, granting that P can employ some linguistic conventions to make comparisons between sensations, P could establish a workable language in which he successfully identifies and refers to private experiences without, of course, conclusively verifying or being sure of his uses of words. There are, of course, other problems with P's "language," one of which being the question of whether P can make the essential distinction between the practice of naming, for example, and the language rule entailed in that practice. In Chapter 4 we shall analyze P's alleged language at length. The point here is that unless one rules out a weak kind of verification, P's language is not ruled out because of the nature of the subject matter, that is, sensations.[19]

But even if P has and can use rules, why would P apply rules to the context of naming rather than to some other use? This question is obviously unanswerable. But it is not the presupposition of this chapter that naming is a basic function of language, nor is it being argued that given that P has sensations and can function with rules he necessarily will name his sensations. Rather, we are arguing that under the conditions specified, P *can* refer to and name his sensations.

There is, then, at least one counter-instance to the Strong Private Language Argument. Given that one has access to some conventions or patterns for consistently reapplying sounds as words applicable to classes of objects, a language whose sole subject matter is private experiences is not precluded. In Chapter 7 we shall argue that if P's "language" as we have delineated it is a language, it is not a private language, because no rule-guided language (and therefore no language) can be a private language. Here we are merely pointing out that one cannot successfully argue in support of the conclusion that a private language is an absurdity merely on the premise that private experiences, the subject matter for such a language, are improper subjects for linguistic reference.

Such a counter-example to the SPLA also brings into question the Private Phenomenon Argument, since talk about private phenomena is not ruled out simply because the phenomena are *private*, or, as we shall show on other grounds, because a private language is impossible. Malcolm's analysis of the ideas of dreaming illustrates the absurdities to which the Private Phenomenon Argument can needlessly lead and shows that some of the problems with this analysis can be traced to a philosophical fear of talking about a private psychological phenomenon. Even if Malcolm does not identify the meaning of "dream" with the criteria for saying that someone dreamed, it is nevertheless difficult to sort out these two notions in his analysis. For if the concept of dreaming is formed from R's dream impressions and reports, so that a dream is not independent of dream-telling, and if dream-telling itself is a "form of life" beyond which philosophical inquiry ceases, then one wonders how one is to talk about a dream apart from dream-telling except to say that it is a sleeping activity. Any means by which one might isolate the concept of a dream from a report is missing, since according to Malcolm's account one cannot refer to dreams or verify that one has had a dream except through dream-telling.

Moreover, Malcolm's analysis of dreaming cannot account for such activities as sleep-walking, learning while one is asleep, and talking in one's sleep. And by his analysis of the criteria for saying that one dreamed, it would be impossible to say that an animal or a baby dreamed, since they are unable to give accounts of their dreams. Malcolm's criteria for saying that "X is dreaming" are necessarily missing in the cases of infants, animals, and people who cannot speak or otherwise communicate.

I would suggest that Malcolm is held back from going beyond the criteria for dreaming to talking about dreams themselves as distinct phenomena because he would then be treating dreams as private phenomena, so that there would be no means of verifying whether or not one had truly dreamed. Because dreams occur in one's sleep they are not verifiable, even by oneself, except through memories of dreaming. Malcolm thus may fear that a commitment to the possibility that one can *refer* to a private experience apart from its public criteria will commit him to the possibility that the term "dream" has private *meaning* and therefore that "dream" could be a word in a private language. In Chapter 8 we shall show that this fear is unjustified. But by avoiding the former commitment Malcolm cannot get at the phenomenon of dreaming itself apart from dream-telling, and this surely is not adequate to account for what one means by the term "dream." Thus while we can be sympathetic to Malcolm's analysis of dreaming in light of the private language arguments we have discussed in this chapter, the conclusions of the analysis are questionable, since Malcolm has not properly separated dreams from dream-telling.

Problems that allegedly develop when one takes as the starting point of a philosophical analysis an unverifiable private experience cannot be solved merely by trying to avoid the notion of a private experience altogether, although we have presented two examples in contemporary philosophical thinking that have attempted such a solution. In each case it has been seen that one cannot successfully analyze psychological events merely through publicly verifiable terms, because, at least in the instances examined here, it would appear that such analyses do not provide an adequate explanation of the occurrence of, or talk about, these events.

A more satisfactory method of meeting the difficulties of a Humean analysis such as that illustrated in Chapter 2, a method that does not lead to a sort of reductionism in analyses of psychological phenomena, is arrived at, I think, through a more thorough examination of the private language arguments. It may be possible to avoid many of the problems encountered in a Humean approach by showing that arguments that a private language is impossible do not necessarily lead to the conclusion that a private experience is impossible. In the remainder of this chapter and in the chapters to follow we shall make such arguments. In Chapter 8 we shall show how reference to private experiences *is* possible without committing oneself to a private language.

V

Bernard Gert once argued that a private language is exhaustively defined as the "language that would result if one could create language simply by means of a private ostensive definition."[20] In a more recent article Gert has elaborated on this claim. Gert argues that what Wittgenstein means by a private language consists solely of a version of PL_a. While Wittgenstein does not commit himself to the thesis that there are private sensations, according to Gert's reading of Wittgenstein, if a private language makes sense, it must be a language constructed by the association of a sound with an immediate private sensation. The essential characteristic of such a language is that individual words refer to immediate sensations. The so-called language is to be created solely from sound (or mark)-sensation associations such that the meanings of the words so constructed are derived from, and identified with, their references. The speaker of such a language uses no external references, she has no prior conception of what the sensations in question are, nor does she use language rules derived from any other language she knows. Therefore, although the language so derived is intelligible to its creator-speaker, she cannot translate or explain this language to anyone else, because the meanings as well as the references are unintelligible to anyone but the speaker. If such a language were translatable, it would no longer be a private language.[21]

Gert's preoccupation with PL_a may be an overstatement of all that is involved in the private language arguments, since a number of contemporary commentators have understood the definition differently. Nevertheless Gert forces us to reexamine Wittgenstein's own private language arguments and thus take into account the origin of the variety of these arguments that have been derived from his work. It is certainly true that Wittgenstein's arguments against the possibility of a private language were formulated at least in part to show that private ostensive definition in the form of associating a sound with a particular sensation is not a possible *starting place* for the construction, development, or learning of a language. This is what we shall call the Weak Private Language Argument (WPLA). This position does not rule out the possibility of talking about and referring to private phenomena. Rather, the contention is merely that a language cannot be constructed or develop *in the first instance* merely from trying to define ostensively private phenomena such as one's sensations.

To understand what is at stake in this argument we must first clarify what one means by the terms *ostensive definition, primitive ostensive definition,* and *private ostensive definition.* Often one means by ostensive definition the process of attaching sounds as names to classes of phenomena. This is done by associating a sound with a particular phenomenon through some means of direct referring such as pointing and then reinforcing the association by applying the same sound to similar phenomena through the same referring device. We shall call this ordinary ostensive definition. What is usually meant by the term *ostensive learning,* then, is the process through which one is taught (or learns) to use certain sounds as names for certain *kinds* of phenomena through some repeatable direct sound-phenomenon referring method such as pointing.

At least part of making ostensive definitions consists in merely uttering a sound or making a sign in the presence of a particular, whereupon the phenomenon is christened, and one may define ostensive definition merely as this limited activity. In this instance, to use Bertrand Russell's terminology, a "particular particular" is given a "proper name" or a "logically proper name."[22] We shall call this primitive ostensive definition, where the uttered sound denotes merely the immediate particular or object with which one is acquainted at the moment. "And in that it has a very odd property for a proper name, namely that it seldom means the same thing two moments running and does not mean the same thing to the speaker and to the hearer."[23] Hence the same sound can be reapplied at random to succeeding objects to which one is later acquainted, and there is no reason why any sound cannot be a "logically proper name" (in the Russellian sense of "logically proper") for any particular.

What is meant by private ostensive definition is the association of a sound or a sign with a private phenomenon or event perceivable or knowable only to the person making the association, either by primitive ostensive definition or by ordinary ostensive definition. What is involved in the Weak Private Language Argument, then, is either (1) that one cannot derive a language merely from making private primitive sound-sensation associations, or (2) that, in general, one cannot derive a language from private (ordinary) ostensive definition.

It is sometimes suggested that language is learned from making a series of primitive ostensive definitions from which the pupil acquires the ability to refer to a number of similar objects or classes or phenomena with the same sound. But let us attempt to construct a language from private primitive ostensive definitions. In this case R must derive words from particular sound-sensation associations. Let us suppose that under these conditions R experiences a sensation and on its occurrence she utters a sound and christens the sensation with the logically proper name "pain." When R experiences a second sensation she may utter the same sound or another sound and thereby christen the second sensation. Subsequently, R calls attention to each momentary feeling as it occurs by uttering a series of sounds which become proper names for a series of sensations that she experiences. But the idea of reapplying a sound consistently or correctly to certain kinds of sensations makes no sense in this case. By the nature of the "object" (i.e., a momentary particular as defined in this example) R cannot reapply a sound consistently as an ordinary name because the numerically identical named object does not and cannot reappear. Nor has R any rules with which to associate *similar* sensations with the same sound. Therefore, in merely trying to form a language from primitive ostensive definitions any sound-sensation association could be made and would be all right, since each sound is associated only to a particular momentary sensation, and the resulting "language" is merely a series of unrelated sounds. In this "language" some sounds may reoccur as names of similar or different sensations or not reoccur at all. The "words" in this proposed language could apply to anything, for they do not denote kinds or classes of sensations. In these circumstances R could develop no method for distinguishing one kind of sensation from another, because R has no criteria for what counts as a correct or an incorrect association. "Ostensive definition cannot be the basis of language for it presupposes knowledge of the use of similar words."[24] Neither R nor anyone else could understand from one moment to the next to what a particular sound would apply. This "language," then, would be incomprehensible to everyone including R.

Obviously, then, if by "ostensive definition" one means "primitive ostensive definition," Wittgenstein would reject the idea that a private language could develop this way. Notice, however, that this argument applies to the formation of *any* language, since primitive ostensive definition, whether or not it is private, cannot be the basis for developing or constructing any sorts of words.

The argument that private primitive ostensive definition cannot provide the basis for language, language learning, or language development is not entirely a specious argument, however. Private primitive ostensive definition attempts to derive references and meanings solely from sound-sensation associations. If such definitions are not basic to language, then either language does not consist merely in giving names to phenomena, or the naming process must be explicated differently. Any phenomenalist approach that takes the language of sensations to be basic when that language is constructed from primitive private ostensive definition is thereby in question, and bringing such theories into question is at least part of Wittgenstein's aim in developing the private language arguments.[25] For example, a Humean approach that attempts to begin philosophical analysis merely from distinct impressions and ideas is thereby precluded as a fruitful philosophical methodology.

Wittgenstein wants to carry the attack on ostensive definition beyond primitive ostensive definition, for he questions the idea that "learning language consists in giving names to objects."[26] Theories of ostensive definition seem to focus on naming as basic to language. But Wittgenstein says that "[n]aming appears as a *queer* connection of a word with an object."[27] This is because "[a] great deal of stage-setting in the language is presupposed if the mere act of naming is to make sense."[28] In other words, ostensive definitions are meaningful only after one has learned certain language skills and only in a context of these skills.[29] To put the point simply, in order to learn by ostensive definition, the pupil must have some at least implicit grasp of an associative principle entailed in the defining process. The pupil must be able to interpret the ostensive associative link (e.g., pointing) as a link between sound and object and as a link that may be repeated in other, similar situations. Otherwise, the pupil might misinterpret the pointer or not understand that principle of making definitions at all. In avoiding further misunderstanding the pupil needs also to grasp what "sortal" is involved, that is, what sort of object is being a defined, for example, a shape, a color, or an object.[30] What Wittgenstein wants to show is that ostensive definition is not basic to language learning, being prompted, at a minimum, by the linguistic framework of associative rules. Think, for example, of how one teaches a child colors. One often points to various colored shapes, encouraging the child to apply color sounds, (e.g., red, green, etc.). But until the child understands that pointing links a sound (e.g., red) with a quality of an object the learning process does not progress. Second, the child must grasp that this process is iterative. Third, so as not to confuse a red chair with a red dress, the child must grasp the defining sortal (e.g., color in this case). This is not to argue that a child is aware of these connections and can explain all of these associations. But a child must be functionally able to use these principles or rules in order to learn by ostensive definition. If this is what one means by the term "ostensive definition," then associative rules are basic to such definitions.

More is at stake in making ordinary ostensive definitions than merely the presence or knowledge of rules for association. Ostensive definitions are made in a context. There is a nexus of rules entailed in making ostensive definitions and learning to name. Wittgenstein calls this nexus of rules in a context "this wider horizon of related rule-governed activities . . . a *language-game.*"[31] "Naming appears as a *queer* connection of a word with an object" because it is not merely the linking of a sound with a class of phenomena through a rule (e.g., pointing) that takes place. The context of the reference is also important. This explains Wittgenstein's claim that "an ostensive definition can be variously interpreted in *every* case . . ."[32] and "how he 'takes' the definition is seen in the use that he makes of the word defined."[33] The nexus of rules and their use in a particular context, what Wittgenstein calls a language-game,[34] regulates the interpretation, and this, of course, varies with each context.

To give an illustration, according to what we know, early Greeks had what speakers of English would think of as strange uses of color words. A so-called color word did not refer merely to a hue as color words in English supposedly do, but each word was connected with a family of associations not ordinarily connected with color.

> For example, the word . . . [for] the "green" of Euripides' blood carries with it associations with moisture, fresh vegetation, and youth, and even fear. We could say: its sense is a fusion of such associations.[35]

Unless one understands these kinds of associations Greek uses of color words are hard to translate. Even in English, however, color words have different connotations depending on the context in which they are used. An alien translator who thought she understood the reference of the color word "blue" might have difficulty with phrases such as, "I am blue," "I am blue with cold," "blue Monday," or "the blues." In defining "blue" by ostensive association the language-game in which the word is used as well as the associate rule and sortal all play roles in the interpretation of "blue" in each context, and in each context "blue" has a somewhat different meaning.

Wittgenstein's point is that if one means by (private) ostensive definition ordinary (private) ostensive definition, then given that P could use or develop some patterns to distinguish his sensations and memories in such a way that he could identify and hence ostensively apply the same sound repeatedly to similar sensations and distinguish these from different kinds of sensations, and if, using these rules P could develop his own "language-game" of ostensive definition, P could construct a language about his sensations through making ordinary private ostensive definitions. But using ordinary ostensive definitions depends on "training," that is, on being able to grasp a nexus of rules or referring tools such as pointing, and these are conceptually prior to the sound-phenomenon association. Hume noticed this, and he devised his "principles of association" to explain how ostensive definition could take place. Thus while one can develop a language from ordinary ostensive definitions, one can do so only if one already has or can use or comprehend some associative rules in particular contexts. Is such a language a private language? Can one be a Rule Skeptic? Only if one can develop private associative rules and/or private language-games. In Chapters 6 and 7 we shall see whether this is possible.

VI

The upshot of this discussion for the Weak Private Language Argument is as follows. It is clear from Wittgenstein's extensive discussion of ostensive definitions that no sound can gather meaning as a word merely from primitive ostensive definition. The Weak Private Language Argument is valid if one means by "private ostensive definition" "private primitive ostensive definition," where the "objects" out of which one is trying to form a language are momentary sensations or impressions treated as such. No language can develop merely from simple associations of sounds with particular momentary sensations, because the possibility of consistently reapplying sounds as words referring to classes of objects is necessarily missing in this case. These arguments are arguments against the privacy of sensation language derived from private primitive ostensive definition. As we noted earlier, such a conclusion is important for bringing into question philosophical theories that start their analyses from such a position. However, this conclusion follows almost immediately and fairly obviously from the definitions of "primitive ostensive definition" and "logically proper name." Moreover, it is a general argument applying to the development of any language whatsoever and therefore is not merely an attack on *private* language.

In the case of private ordinary ostensive definition, by using associative patterns or referring to rules in the context of a language-game one *can* form a language from these kinds of associations. This is because ostensive association is not basic to language learning, being preempted by rules of association and the interpretative context or language-game in which they appear. This form of the Weak Private Language Argument, then, reverts to the question of whether or not one can develop private rules and/or whether the notion of a private language-game makes sense, that is, whether or not it is possible to construct *any* language that is unintelligible to others.

It could be surmised that if one cannot construct a private language from private primitive ostensive definition, this eliminates the possibility of any sort of private language, since private meanings could not be established merely through primitive sound-sensation associations. Since the latter is impossible, a private language, that is, a language that is unintelligible to anyone but its speaker, is thereby impossible. The meaning of a word depends on its use, a use that cannot be established merely by private associations. In Chapter 7 I shall agree with the conclusion that a private language of any sort is impossible. But merely because one cannot construct a language from private primitive ostensive definition does not, in itself, preclude the possibility of any private language. Whether Wittgenstein thought that this was the case is unclear. But because so many versions of the private language argument have been generated from Wittgenstein's references, it is important to continue the analysis.

VII

One cannot develop a language merely from ostensive definition or private ostensive associations. But the impossibility of a private language developed from ostensive definition does not entail logical behaviorism. That a language cannot, in principle, be incomprehensible to anyone but its speaker does not exclude reference to, or denotation of, phenomena that are experienced by only one person. Private languages and private phenomena are not in the same category. The exclusion or inclusion of one does not have much to do with the exclusion or inclusion of the other. These private language arguments enable us to sacrifice the counter-intuitive claim that in principle one cannot understand the language of another. Yet they do not entail giving up one's commonsense belief that at least some sensations, feelings, and psychological phenomena are peculiarly and privately one's own, although the relationship between language and these phenomena will have to be reestablished on other grounds.

What is also evident is that formulations of the private language argument that focus solely on the subject matter of a language are inadequate to deal with all the possibilities of a private language. The privacy of the subject matter of a language such as PL_a, PL_b, or PL_d is not a necessary condition for the privacy of PL_a, PL_b, or PL_d as *languages*. If PL_a and PL_b are private languages it is not because of their subject matter, but rather because of the way they are constructed. Since the only "peculiar" characteristic of PL_d is that its subject matter is private experiences, PL_d is not thereby necessarily a private language. Therefore, a number of philosophers contend, the problem with the idea of a private language lies primarily not with the proposed subject matter of such a hypothetical language, but with its lack of sociability. We shall discuss these theses in Chapters 4 and 5. Still other philosophers question the idea of a private language through an analysis of Wittgenstein's notions of language-game and language rule. In Chapters 6 and 7 we shall consider these views.

Notes

1. Fogelin, *Wittgenstein*, pp. 153–171.
2. Kenny, *Wittgenstein*, pp. 191–192.
3. On this point see Kenny, *Wittgenstein*, pp. 191–193, and Stewart Candlish, "The Real Private Language Argument," *Philosophy* 55 (1980): pp. 85–94.
4. This kind of argument was originally defended by Norman Malcolm, V. C. Chappell, and others. See Norman Malcolm, "Wittgenstein's *Philosophical Investigations*," *Philosophical Review* 63 (1954), reprinted in Norman Malcolm, *Knowledge and Certainty* (Englewood Cliffs, NJ: Prentice-Hall, 1963), pp. 96–129; Norman Malcolm, "Knowledge of Other Minds," *Journal of Philosophy* 55 (1958), reprinted in *Knowledge and Certainty*, pp. 130–140; and V. C. Chappell, "'The Private-Language Argument'—Comments," in *Knowledge and Experience*, ed. C. D. Rollins (Pittsburgh, PA: University of Pittsburgh Press), pp. 106–118. These philosophers claim that what is missing are both (a) proper kinds of objects to construct a language and (b) language rules.

However, we are justified in simplifying the argument for our purposes here, because these thinkers claim that even with language rules one cannot create a language merely from private experiences.

5. Chappell, "'The Private-Language Argument'—Comments," p. 108, my italics.
6. Malcolm, "Wittgenstein's *Philosophical Investigations*," p. 100.
7. Ibid., pp. 96–129.
8. V. C. Chappell, Introduction to *The Philosophy of Mind*, ed. V. C. Chappell (Englewood Cliffs, NJ: Prentice-Hall, 1962), p. 13.
9. Malcolm, "Wittgenstein's *Philosophical Investigations*," p. 105 footnote, added to original essay.
10. Chappell, Introduction, p. 13.
11. Malcolm, "Knowledge of Other Minds," p. 136.
12. Chappell, Introduction, p. 13.
13. Norman Malcolm, *Dreaming* (London: Routledge & Kegan Paul, 1959), p. 4, quoted from R. M. Yost, Jr., and D. Kalish, "Miss Macdonald on Sleeping and Waking," *Philosophical Quarterly* 5 (1955): 118. Malcolm inverted the order of the quotation from the original.
14. Malcolm, *Dreaming*, p. 79.
15. Ibid., p. 60.
16. Ibid.
17. Ibid., p. 87.
18. In Chapters 4 and 7 we shall discuss the problem of constructing a language when one has only "think-rules." Here we are merely arguing that such a language is a possibility given the subject matter of the language.
19. In Chapter 4 P's language is ruled out because of the absence of social practices, but that argument rules out *any* language and not merely PL_a.
20. Bernard Gert, "Wittgenstein and Private Language," abstract of a paper presented to the American Philosophical Association Meetings, *Journal of Philosophy* 61 (1964): 700. A revised version of this paper was published under the title "Wittgenstein's Private Language Arguments," *Synthese* 68 (1986): 409–419.
21. Gert, "Wittgenstein's Private Language Arguments," pp. 409–419.
22. Bertrand Russell, *Logic and Knowledge*, ed. Robert C. Marsh (London: George Allen and Unwin, 1956), pp. 198–202.
23. Ibid., p. 201.
24. Gert, "Wittgenstein's Private Language Arguments," p. 414.
25. Ibid., pp. 418–419.
26. Wittgenstein, *PI*, §26.
27. Ibid., §38.
28. Ibid., §257.
29. See Fogelin, *Wittgenstein*, p. 106.
30. Wittgenstein, *PI* §33–35. Saul Kripke claims that sortals are not important to ostensive definition according to Wittgenstein, and that one can make ostensive definitions without them. This may be true, but that is not Wittgenstein's point. See Kripke, *Wittgenstein on Rules and Private Language*, p. 84n.
31. Hintikka and Hintikka, *Investigating Wittgenstein*, p. 189.
32. Wittgenstein, *PI* §28.

33. Ibid., §29.
34. "What is the relation between name and thing named?- Well, what *is* it? Look at language-game (2) or another one: there you can see the sort of thing this relation consists in." *PI* §37.
35. Quoted from Dancy, "Alien Concepts," p. 297.

4

"'Obeying a Rule' Is a Practice"

The arguments of Chapter 3 have shown that (a) one cannot develop a language merely from associating sounds with sensations, and (b) the use of ostensive definition and private ostensive definition presuppose at least implicit knowledge of the concept of naming and other simple grammatical rules. Nevertheless, in connection with the analysis of the Strong Private Language Argument we said that given that a man, P, had or could develop some patterns or conventions for applying sounds as repeatable words in a variety of situations, it is not impossible that P could develop a language, the subject matter of which was his private experiences.

It is now the task of this chapter to consider the possibility of P's language from another perspective, that of PL_e, a language developed by one person in physical or linguistic isolation from any other person or community of persons. The discussion of this possibility will entail a careful analysis of the possibility of PL_e as well as an analysis of the roles of community and community agreement, social practice, and consensus in language development and language use. We shall refer to positions that defend the thesis that a community, a social practice, or a consensus is necessary for language as Community Views of language, and arguments that defend this view against the position that a language, PL_e, could develop in linguistic or physical isolation, as the Community Arguments (CPLA).

Community Views of language and the private language arguments they give rise to raise some important issues. If language is based on habit, consensus, or conventions, then truth conditions, too, are formulated on these grounds. Moreover, it could be the case that two communities, A and B, had such incommensurable social practices that each developed a language that could not be understood by the other. Thus

67

while it is impossible for one person to develop a language in isolation, different societies could do so. Community Views, then, challenge forms of realism, they redefine the nature of truth, and they are consistent with linguistic relativism. These dramatic conclusions result from the Community Private Language Arguments. Consequently such arguments must be examined most scrupulously not merely because they question the idea of a private language, but more importantly because of the types of conclusions that are alleged to follow from their adoption.

There are at least four forms of a Community View of language, each of which is based on a similar argument against a private language. First, according to at least one version of this view,

> Wittgenstein's point [in the private language arguments] . . . is a . . . radical one, that what it is for a person to be following a rule, even individually, cannot ultimately be explained without reference to some community.[1]

A person, R, by herself in physical or linguistic isolation cannot develop a language, because criteria for distinguishing what R thinks is a correct use from what is a correct use are missing.[2] A second form contends that because language develops from the customs, habits, and dispositions of a community, a private language makes no sense. A third version argues that the social nature of human beings precludes the development of any language in social isolation. A fourth focuses on Wittgenstein's alleged conventionalism, a conventionalism that implies reading Wittgenstein as an epistemological antirealist. This view argues in brief that since the truth-relationship of a word to its referent (or, more broadly, of language to the world) cannot be established, community agreement is necessary for consensus about what is true or false and thus for there to be language at all.

In this chapter I shall challenge some of the Community Views of language. I shall argue that Community Views are not without textual support in the *Philosophical Investigations*, but the interpretation of these texts is misdirected. Empirically it may be the case that a language "would lose its point outside a community that generally agrees in its practices,"[3] as those who hold a Community View conclude. Nevertheless, I shall argue that community agreements do not form the bedrock or the court of last appeal in language formation, rule following, or evaluation, as some proponents of a Community View contend. This is probably not exactly what Wittgenstein meant by a "form of life," and even if it were, such a position commits us to a consensus-based theory of language which is, at best, implausible. Such a thesis allows the possibility of mutually incomprehensible languages, a possibility inconsistent with the private language arguments. Moreover, the antirealist conventionalism derived from some forms of a Community View has its own difficulties as well. Conventionalism, then, while possibly having merit on other grounds, can neither be derived from, nor used in support of, private language arguments.

I

A Community View comes out of worries about language, language rules, and rule following and develops at least in part from a particular interpretation of Wittgenstein's position about the following. First, Wittgenstein explicitly states,

> It is not possible that there should have been only one occasion on which someone obeyed a rule . . . To obey a rule, make a report, . . . are *customs* (uses, institutions).[4] . . . And hence also "obeying a rule" is a practice.[5]

"Practice" in this context could mean a social practice. Thus according to a Community View, Wittgenstein thought that rules and rule following were rooted in social practices or customs.

Second, Wittgenstein often talks about the indeterminateness of rule-following. For example, in §84 he says that "the application of a word is not everywhere bounded by rules"; or in §142, "It is only in normal cases that the use of a word is clearly prescribed." If one is unsure about "how to go on," or if a number of interpretations of a rule count as "correct," this leads to a skepticism about rule-following, a skepticism that could be resolved with the thesis that social agreements determine what counts or should count as correctness in rule-following.

Third, from Wittgenstein's edict that "to *think* one is obeying a rule is not to obey a rule"[6] most communitarians adopt the position that I cannot know merely from my own case whether I am following a rule or only think I am. That is, I cannot know whether or not I am following a rule correctly even if I intend to do so, because such intentions alone cannot provide independent criteria for such evaluations. Accordingly, a community provides the criteria for ratification of rule applications so that the distinction between rules, following a rule, and think-rules can be made.

Fourth, Wittgenstein talks in some places as if states of mind are dispositions.[7] Language seems to reflect dispositions and habits. But according to the private language arguments, these cannot be reflections merely of my dispositions and habits. Thus language derives from, and reflects, the dispositions and habits of a community. Fifth, Wittgenstein says that "When I obey a rule, I do not choose. I obey the rule *blindly*."[8] Thus a community provides the background conditions that allow these "blind" habits to develop.

Finally, according to Wittgenstein, "If I have exhausted the justifications I have reached bedrock, and my spade is turned."[9] Because of the private language arguments, the "bedrock" cannot be some sort of internal foundational basis such as impressions or sense data. So community agreements are likely candidates. They form the bedrock, the background for language and rule-following beyond which one cannot go further. In what follows we shall see how these sorts of textual interpretations are used to justify certain Community Views and what problems develop with these interpretations.

II

As we saw in Chapter 3, the original private language arguments defined a private language as a language developed merely from private ostensive associations of sounds with sensations (private ostensive definition). It was then argued that such a language is impossible. Community Views do not dispute these arguments, but they focus their attention on a peculiar kind of private language, a language developed by one person in physical or linguistic isolation from any other person or a community of persons.

> Whatever noises a linguistically isolated individual might make, they would not count as a "language." In this sense a "private language" is a chimera, for language is always a social activity involving the rules that only a social situation can provide. This general conclusion seems to be completely established by Wittgenstein.[10]

The difficulty, as we shall see, is with the meaning of the term "linguistically isolated." It could be that a person has been brought up (or raised herself) in complete solitude. This person, call her Susan Crusoe, differs from her brother because in addition to being physically isolated as Robinson was, Susan has no conception of the notion of a rule. Although she might utter sounds often in the presence of sensations and physical objects, and indeed, Susan might repeat the same sound when a similar sensation of the same physical object reappeared, she has no notion of "correctness" or "incorrectness." Susan can perhaps remember and reidentify similar objects, but she cannot refer to them or compare them to other objects, because she lacks the "conceptual equipment" to do so. Obviously, under these conditions, Susan cannot develop a language.

A more interesting question is whether, at least in theory, Susan *could* develop her own language rules in linguistic isolation, and, if she could, would she then develop a language? Here the question is whether or not *any* sort of language could be developed by an isolated individual in the absence of a community or a social practice. Because Wittgenstein says that "To obey a rule, to make a report . . . are *customs* (uses, institutions)," it is often concluded that the notion of a rule, and thus language, depends on community custom and agreement, without which no person living in solitude could develop language.

Let us imagine that Robinson Crusoe (in physical isolation) tries to construct a language about his sensations. The problem for Robinson is not that he cannot remember whether or not he reassociated correctly a sound S with a sensation (Susan's problem), but rather whether or not there was a genuine "correct connection" or correct use in the first place. In order for a correct use to be established so that Robinson can truly name his sensations, the following conditions must be satisfied:

(i)   Robinson must understand what counts as thinking he is using a sign, S, correctly,
(ii) He must understand what counts as using S correctly, and
(iii) He must be able to distinguish (i) from (ii), that is, there must be criteria for the correct use of S that are not identical with the criteria for thinking one is using S correctly.[11]

One of Robinson's difficulties when he is developing a language of his sensations by himself is that he appears to have no way to distinguish what he thinks is a correct use of S from what is one. He merely has a series of think-rules. This could be what Wittgenstein means by his statement, "As if someone were to buy several copies of the morning paper to assure himself that what it said was true,"[12] because Robinson can only compare what he *thinks* is correct against another think-correct rule without ever having independent standards by which he can evaluate these. It follows that Robinson cannot develop a language about his physical surroundings either. His only criteria for correctness are what he *thinks* are correct applications of the sound "tree," for example, to attach to what he thinks are similar objects.

If a language is "a collection of correct uses,"[13] only a community can provide the independent criteria to establish correctness, because only in a community can a speaker compare (i) with (ii), by using the community's criterion for correctness of the application of the sign S. Notice that even if Susan or Robinson has some sort of notion of a rule, neither seems to have criteria independent of their own think-rules to verify that they are "going on in the same way." So neither could develop a language about their sensations or any sort of language at all by themselves.[14]

One might want to compare this analysis with some of the private language arguments we discussed in Chapter 3. The Strong Private Language Argument contended that the problem in trying to develop a private language was with the sorts of "object" one had (e.g., sensations) as subject matter for such a language. The problem with developing a private language in this instance is with the notion of criterion. One needs to have independent criteria in order to confirm or verify that the rule or rules one thinks one is using are correct ones. A community provides such criteria for rules and rule-following so that one can distinguish what one thinks is a rule for naming, for example, from what the community stipulates as the correct rule.[15]

There is a response to this argument. If a community can set up its own "objective" criteria or rules and agree on "correctness of use," there is no reason why Robinson cannot set up his own "objective" rules in dialogue with himself to evaluate his think-rules and their applications.[16] If Robinson has and can use his own think-rules, there is no justification for saying that he cannot set up his own rule-rules as well, at least according to this scheme. To do this Robinson could set aside some of his think-rules as criteria or standards. Then with each new think-rule-following application Robinson could compare what he was doing in a particular instance with the think-rule he had set aside as the standard. In that way Robinson, just like a community, could distinguish between thinking he was following a think-rule and actually doing so. If others came to Robinson's island they might dispute with him about his uses of words, but this could also occur when a particular community met other communities. So if a community can create agreements about rule-following, it follows that one person in physical isolation can do so as well.

III

The foregoing analysis, however, does not defeat a Community View. We have assumed that Robinson has or can develop think-rules and that within his set of think-rules Robinson can set some aside to function as rule-rules. This assumption is short-sighted. The difficulty with the assumption is not that we have not distinguished between following a rule and thinking one is following a rule, nor is our claim that Robinson is able to make that distinction by setting aside some as criteria to gauge his think-rule-following activities problematic. The difficulty is that we have overlooked the distinction between an application of a rule, that is, following a rule on a particular occasion (or thinking one has), and the rule itself. What Robinson is doing is "thinking-he-is-following-a-rule." Robinson might be able to set aside think-rule applications as prototypes for other subsequent *applications* (rule-following activities). But is he able to grasp the *rules* or even think-rules underlying his applications? Even if Robinson sets aside some think-rule applications to function as evaluative standards, these are not rules but merely interpretations of rules. So even if Robinson appears to distinguish between thinking he is following a rule and actually doing so, we have not shown that he has a notion of a *rule*, a notion that is needed to evaluate his various interpretations. Robinson's problem concerns the existence of rules, not their applications, and it is rules, not their applications, that Robinson apparently lacks.[17]

These sorts of arguments are illustrative of what I would call a Dispositional Community View. Wittgenstein's position on rule-following (and hence his private language arguments) are well expressed in §199 and §202. "'Obeying a rule' is a practice" could be read to mean that the existence of rules and their applications (following or obeying rules) evolves out of actual and continuing practices and customs. The notion of a practice entails agreement with, or consensus of, a community.

> . . . [O]nly by appealing to the fact that the genuine rule-follower agrees in his reactions to examples with the members of some community can we say what distinguishes him from someone who falsely thinks he is following a rule.[18]

Wittgenstein's claim that "[h]ence it is not possible to obey a rule privately"[19] is interpreted to mean that a person in isolation cannot distinguish what she thinks to be a rule from what *are* rules because there is no community to provide the latter. Without these community-generated rules as criteria for evaluating rule-following, an individual would have no restrictions on her particular think-rule-following habits. Any grammatical formation and any sort of referring device could count as a language rule, and thus none would formulate itself or be formulated by the speaker as consistent reusable criteria for rule-following. Without established practices for correctness and incorrectness, practices only developed in social agreement, an individual in isolation is lacking rules, so she cannot distinguish correct from incorrect uses of sounds.

Our friend Robinson has an impression he is following a rule. Even if he sets aside some of these impressions as "criteria" to judge each subsequent impression, he has no notion of a rule independent of these rule-following activities through which he can judge his impressions. Therefore Robinson may think he is following a rule correctly, but he has no justification for his belief.[20] Robinson may correct his errors in rule-following only from other applications, the ones he has set aside. But Robinson does not know whether or not he is *really* following a rule correctly because he has no grasp of independent rules. Genuine rules impose restrictions that Robinson's situation appears to lack. It is only in a community or a social context where language rules can be developed as independent criteria or standards that Robinson could sort out his applications, that is, his think-rule-following activities, from actual rule-following. This is because only in this sort of context will he have at hand the rule or rules that his applications exemplify or fail to exemplify to verify that he is truly following a rule.

The crux of this explanation of Wittgenstein is as follows. Through social practices, habits, and dispositions communities create "sameness-establishing conventions."[21] These are not natural relations but are considered "natural" by the community. Community dispositions and habits are the authority for sameness-establishing conventions, including language rules. This bottom-line consensus is what Wittgenstein means by a "form of life" or "bedrock" beyond which one cannot question, according to this explication. While one can question the application of a rule (e.g., Does 1010 follow from 1002, 1004, 1006, etc.?), at its most basic level one cannot question the rule itself or the consensus of the community concerning the rules it adopts. Thus, it is contended, a language developed in physical or linguistic isolation is impossible, and neither Robinson nor Susan Crusoe can develop language.

One of the most serious difficulties with the foregoing account is the dispositional analysis of rules. This view plays down one important characteristic of rules, namely their normative or prescriptive character. It is not merely that we can explain our behavior or language in terms of rules, but also that rules set up criteria for how one should act or speak. Rules are not merely descriptive of what we are disposed to do. They also set up normative standards of what we should do and how we should go on.[22] In response, one might argue that rules *develop* out of community dispositions, habits, and agreements and then *become* normative standards for individual behavior and language use. But this leaves us with no means by which rules of a community themselves can be evaluated or changed, since they, then, are "forms of life." We shall return to that issue later in the chapter.

There is another problem with a Dispositional Theory. One of the reasons for holding a Dispositional Community View is to explain why the notion of a private language is impossible. Community agreements and social consensus allegedly set up criteria for rules and rule following that are independent of my particular think-rule-application criteria to which I subject my own dispositions. Yet if language rules express or reflect community dispositions, why cannot a person in isolation develop rules from her dispositions? Why are communitarian rules better or more valid than one person's dispositional think-rules she has created in isolation? Is it because we find ourselves in agreement that the communitarian account of rules is "better" or more justified as an account of rules and rule-following? Or has the Dispositional View slipped a strong verification requirement, namely, that my think-rules cannot function as rules unless they are publicly acceptable or verified by the agreement of the community?[23] It is claimed that social agreements about rules are sufficient to establish genuine criteria (i.e., rules) for rule-following. What I am arguing is that given dispositional arguments, a community is in no better position than Robinson. Conversely, if a community can develop or grasp a notion of a rule that functions normatively rather than merely habitually, then an individual can do so too. At least it has been demonstrated that the latter is not impossible. For if a community can set aside some of its dispositions and habits as *norms*, that is, as objective criteria or rules as distinguished from interpretations, then there is no reason that Robinson could not formulate at least think-rules from what he thought were correct applications as well. Whether either Robinson or a community could come up with the notion of a rule is a subject for another chapter. What is essential for a community, for Robinson, or even for Susan (in linguistic isolation), if they are to develop a language, is that each has, or can develop, a notion of a rule and distinguish rules from rule-following, applications, or interpretations. What has not been shown is that a community is necessary and/or sufficient for such development. If rules merely reflect community dispositions, then the community is in the same position as a physically isolated person. It has merely its dispositional think-rule applications but no normative criteria for correctness, that is, rules. As we argued, if Robinson simply follows his own dispositions, he will fall into the trap of "'obeying a rule' privately," that is, of not distinguishing what he thinks to be a correct application of a rule (his inclinations) from what are rules and norms. To distinguish rule-following from think-rule-following what Robinson needs to do is to set up normative standards that function independently of his dispositions and intentions to which he can appeal in evaluating each application of signs to sensations and other phenomena. But of course if rules are simply dispositions or habits there is no reason why Robinson's think-rule applications are not as viable as candidates for rules as a community's dispositions.[24]

Robinson's second problem, one will recall, was that even if he sets aside some of his think-rule-following as "standards," what he has set aside are merely applications, not the normative criteria, that is, the rules themselves. Similarly, the community, having derived its so-called rules from dispositions and habits, has at hand only its applications. Since, according to a Dispositional Community View, a community cannot evaluate its own rule following, it, like Robinson, lacks *rules*, that is, standards, to evaluate their dispositions.

The Dispositional View, then, has two difficulties. First, it has not shown that a person in isolation could not develop "objective" think-rule applications and thereby distinguish between thinking he was following a rule and actually doing so. Second, if rules are derived from dispositions and habits, a community is no better off than Robinson, for it, too, has merely applications, interpretations, or rule-following, but no rules. Appealing to Wittgenstein's declaration that "'obeying a rule' is a practice," a Community View attempts to show that rules and genuine rule-following cannot occur or develop at all except in the atmosphere of a community. To defend this thesis, one would have to show that the nature of a rule is such that rules can develop only in a social context. But what does Wittgenstein mean by "'obeying a rule' is a practice"? It is true that rules are not unique sorts of phenomena that occur only once. Rules are formal criteria or standards for organizing, evaluating, and continuing a variety of activities or behaviors. A rule is a formal procedural mechanism whose very structure invites repetition. A rule is a way of acting, doing, or speaking that has a variety of applications in different contexts. These contexts are what Wittgenstein calls language-games. A language-game is a nexus of linguistic and nonlinguistic rule-governed activities—a locus of interrelated rule-following activities. It is in this sense that "obeying a rule is a practice," for the "practice" is the language-game. It is, then, in this sense that obeying rules are customs, uses of institutions, because rule-following is in a context of a practice, a language-game. But such customs or practices do not necessarily require a community. For "practice" here does not necessarily mean a social practice but refers to the fact that a rule is something that can be applied or interpreted over and over again in a variety of situations or language-games.[25]

Returning to the question of linguistic isolation, it is obvious that if Susan, our person in linguistic isolation, has no notion of a rule, even a think-rule, she cannot and will not develop a language. This is true, but trivially so. However, if one means by a person in linguistic isolation merely a person who has no notion of a community or a society, that person has as good a chance of creating language as a person in physical isolation or as a community. It is at best unclear that a person in isolation, whether it be physical or linguistic isolation, has or can develop even think-rules as distinct from think-rule applications. But whether or not this is the case, a Dispositional View has not shown that a community is in a more propitious linguistic position than someone in isolation. What is needed for any language development is the distinction between rules and their applications. But it is not clear that a community is in a privileged position to provide the conditions for this distinction to be made.[26]

IV

A Community interpretation of the private language arguments has consequences not merely for theories about language and language development but also for a theory of knowledge. This is clearly seen in Crispin Wright's interpretation of the private language arguments that he derives both from his analysis of the *Remarks on the Foundations of Mathematics* and the *Philosophical Investigations*, an interpretation that leads Wright to attribute to Wittgenstein both a Community View of language and a radical conventionalism or epistemological anti-realism, which, Wright argues, are logical outcomes of this interpretation. Wright bases his view on three points: (1) Wittgenstein's anti-individualist epistemology that leads to (2) Wittgenstein's questioning what Wright calls "investigation-independence," and (3) Wittgenstein's claim that "the application of a word is not everywhere bounded by rules."[27]

Wittgenstein's private language arguments attack the notion that one can develop a language, and thus discover or establish truths, in the first instance merely from private ostensive definition. Such a conclusion brings into question the viability of beginning a philosophical analysis from an idiolectic starting point, that is, in trying to begin philosophical analysis merely from what is allegedly indubitably known—for example, one's impressions or sensations. This leads Wittgenstein to the conclusion that "there cannot be such a thing as first-person privileged recognition of the dictates of one's understanding an expression."[28] It follows further that I cannot recognize or verify that I am using an expression or a rule consistently or correctly merely from my own case, because I have no independent criteria for such judgments. Nor do I have any assurance I am using an expression correctly or even whether the expression is true or false. Because an idiolectic starting point is impossible, according to Wittgenstein, Wright postulates that Wittgenstein concludes that it is the community, not an individual, on which one depends for language development, rules, criteria for rule-following, and even truth-conditions.

This interpretation has serious consequences for Wright's view concerning truth and objectivity. Because of Wittgenstein's animadversions against an idiolectic starting point as the basis for philosophy, Wright argues that Wittgenstein is skeptical about what Wright calls "investigation-independence." Investigation-independence, in brief, is the view that "confronted with any decidable, objective issue, there is *already* an answer which—if we investigate the matter fully and correctly—we will arrive at."[29] A decidable statement is objective if it has "investigation-independent truth-value." Because patterns of meaning and language use are not developed independently in an idiolect, and because of the impossibility of ratifying facts or uses of words individually on any objective basis, there is no objectivity of meaning. Thus there is no assurance that what one takes to be facts or truths have any independent validity.

Wright interprets Wittgenstein's open-ended description of rule-following from Wittgenstein's various remarks on the subject including, "an ostensive definition can be variously interpreted in *every* case,"[30] or "It is only in normal cases that the use of a word is clearly prescribed,"

or "When I obey a rule I do not choose. I obey the rule blindly" to mean
that

> . . . the moral of the rule-following considerations was . . . that we
> have to regard correct use, or correct response to the use, of any
> particular sentence on a new occasion as objectively indeterminate; it
> is what competent speakers do—where competence is precisely *not* a
> matter of a disposition to conformity with certain investigation-
> independent facts—which determines the correct use of expressions,
> rather than the other way about.[31]

Thus there is no stability in the patterns of language rules and rule-
following, and what counts as a correct use is decided merely by community consensus.

What is more, if I cannot understand my own patterns of rule-
following, there is no assurance I have understood a communitarian
one.

> So we move towards the idea that understanding an expression is a
> kind of "cottoning on"; that is, a leap, an inspired guess at the pattern
> of application which the instructor is trying to get across.[32]

Even if one grants that community assent provides the basis for correctness of rule-following and thus language use, because one cannot know
from one's own case and because of the indeterminate nature of rule-
following, communal agreement itself is based merely on consensus
from habit rather than on any independent grounds of "objective
correctness,"[33] and it too is indeterminate.

Rule-following practices, then, cannot be ratified. Not only do we not
know whether they conform to investigation-independent facts (or if
they do, one can never know that they do, a point Saul Kripke makes
more succinctly than Wright, as we shall see), but it is also the case,
Wright contends, that rule-following practices are not merely a matter of
conformity to community consensus, since these practices themselves
are somewhat indeterminate or "blind." Therefore, according to Wright,
one cannot describe a practice systematically because "at any particular
stage [a practice] may go in *any* direction without betrayal of its character. There is simply nothing *there* systematically to be described."[34]

The upshot of this sort of Community View is twofold. First, although
no language can be developed by a person in isolation from a community, one cannot evaluate the community practices that are the source of
language. One cannot say "a community goes right or wrong in accepting

a particular verdict on a particular decidable question; rather, it just goes."[35] Because linguistic practices are both based on community assent and authority and are at the same time somewhat indeterminate, one cannot evaluate the consensus itself, that is, there is no way to follow a rule or grasp a meaning that is not an interpretation. According to our analysis in the preceding section, we would say that a community lacks normative (language) rules. Second, this indeterminate interpretation of the basis for language, language rules, and truth reinforces Wright's claim that there is no independent basis for truth or validity of factual statements apart from what a community thinks are facts or truths, albeit with the proviso that these community agreements are themselves not purely determinate. The result is a repudiation of any pretense of "objectivity of sameness of use."[36] Community consensus provides a background for the development of general language usage that in turn is used to make judgments about individual uses of words and expressions. One cannot penetrate behind community consensus, nor can a community recognize or evaluate the truth or falsity of its own uses of words. Therefore the assumption that community authority is a faithful reflection of the world is unfounded and unverifiable.

This antirealist interpretation of Wittgenstein originates in part from Wright's rightly noticing Wittgenstein's "anti-idiolectic" epistemology. Wittgenstein repeatedly argues against a position that traces knowledge and truth merely to an idiolectic grasp of verifiable impression patterns. This is clearly evident in his attack of ostensive definition as the basis for language learning and language development. Wright, however, has overreacted by ascribing to Wittgenstein an antirealist communitarian conventionalism that disallows truth conditions altogether. Part of this overreaction is due to what I find to be a mistaken interpretation of Wittgenstein's notions of rules and rule-following, in particular, Wright's insistence that rule-following, according to Wittgenstein, is merely following rules "blindly," a view that leads Wright to say that in rule-following one just "goes" and cannot correct or evaluate one's rule-following "cottoning on" habits.

On the contrary, there is at least a modicum of formal determinacy entailed in Wittgenstein's notion of rules as "signposts" which direct (but do not control) rule-following. It is possible "not to go on in the same way" and to be incorrectly following a rule. This is because rule-following and applications or interpretations of rules do not tell the whole story about rules and rule-following. As Wittgenstein says, "The use of the word 'rule' and the use of the word 'same' are interwoven."[37]

While it may be a habit of human nature to "go on in the same way," to go on in a number of disparate similar ways, and even to go on "blindly," these sorts of activities are not indeterminate. They are not totally "blind" because we can study, evaluate, and correct our habits or "goings on." As Wittgenstein says,

> . . . there is a way of grasping a rule which is *not* an *interpretation*, but which is exhibited in what we call "obeying the rule" and "going against it" in actual cases . . . Hence there is an inclination to say "every action according to the rule is an interpretation." But we ought to restrict the term "interpretation" to the substitution of one expression of the rule for another.[38]

One can read this passage to imply that rules are not merely interpretations. To follow a rule is to apply a rule to a particular situation. This specific application is an interpretation of a rule but not identical with it. Thus an individual is not merely dependent on community consensus for guidance in the correction of rules, nor is a community itself merely dependent on its dispositions and habits. Self-correction is possible on both levels even if it is that case that "[w]hen I obey a rule . . . I obey the rule *blindly*" because "there is a way of grasping a rule which is *not* an *interpretation*." This "grasping" is not merely rule-following but involves evaluating the interpretation of the rule itself.

Wright's explication of Wittgenstein leads him to the questionable position of attributing to Wittgenstein a form of antirealism, the obliteration of the normativeness of meaning, and the elimination of the notion that understanding is a grasp of rules and patterns. This reading also implies that the only valid private language arguments are the Community Private Language Arguments and that, in turn, acceptance of those latter arguments entails antirealist conventionalism. However, one can take a middle position between individualistic realism and what I would call a Wrightian antirealist conventionalism, a moderate position more appropriate to Wittgenstein's own view and to what actually is the case. One may construe Wittgenstein's alleged communitarianism as saying that one has membership in a linguistic community where there are a multitude of minds reflecting and sharing linguistic and nonlinguistic practices. But this does not entail assimilation of all understanding under interpretation, because, Wittgenstein says in §201, "there is a way of grasping a rule which is *not* an *interpretation*, but which is exhibited in what we call 'obeying the rule' and 'going against it' in actual cases." Elsewhere, Wittgenstein writes,

If anyone believes that certain concepts are absolutely the right ones, and that having different ones would mean not realizing something that we realize—then let him imagine certain very general facts of nature to be different from what we are used to, and the formation of concepts different from usual ones will become intelligible to him.[39]

So, Wittgenstein is not committed to an identification of meaning with community agreement or consensus, and thus he is not committed to an antirealist interpretation of rule-following.

V

Despite its difficulties, at least one construal of a Community View has been influential in moral philosophy. One version of this nonfoundational epistemology makes an interesting case for moral realism. Wittgenstein is alleged to argue that what is real and true cannot be distinguished from what we call reality and what we hold to be true. Reality, according to this interpretation, is "what is observed by the ideal observer—the person of sound judgement."[40] This point of view, the perspective of the ideal observer, is the perspective stipulatively agreed upon by the community, as "proper" or correct. The stipulated perspective of the ideal observer creates conditions for objectivity and the ground for intellectual and moral authority. Based on community consensus as to what should be real, true, good, or right, the point of view of the ideal observer allows the development of a form of objectivity and designates standards that become the "objective authority" for scientific truth and for moral judgments. This is a form of moral realism because "it asserts the existence of *intellectual authority-relations* in the realm of morals."[41] These authority-relations, developed from the point of view of the ideal observer, form the conditions for making moral judgments, judgments that are made true or false on the basis of this objectified authority. Moral facts, those "facts" that transcend individual value judgments, are just those institutional and community standards established as authoritative, that is, as objectively acceptable to the ideal observer (in that society) as distinct from individual standards and value judgments. Admittedly, "moral facts have a nonmetaphysical way of failing to be, in the collective sense, recognition-transcendent."[42] There is no appeal beyond the linguistic community, but this is because we cannot imagine what such recognition-transcendence would mean. The social and institutionally grounded "objectivity" that distinguishes subjective moral judgments from those with authority is enough to establish a moral realist position.

This is a fascinating argument because it makes a unique case for a form of moral realism from an antirealist perspective. Such an approach, if viable, responds to traditional objections of moral realism by providing actual, verifiable authority-content with which to judge the truth or falsity of a moral judgment without appealing to a form of noncognitivism. It allows us to be moral realists while preserving a form of relativism yet without resorting to either intuitionism or absolutism. But however interesting this thesis is, I argue that it is questionable for the very reasons given for the approach.

Moral realism is often identified with absolutism, the position that there are some objectively real moral principles valid for all human beings or communities of human beings. However, moral realism can be defined more minimally as "a claim that moral judgments are independent of certain mental states."[43] It might appear, then, that a communitarian formulation of moral realism fits this sort of description since, "[O]ur proposed realism explains . . . how the truth-conditions of moral sentences may transcend the recognitional abilities of the individual."[44] But this is not the case. While the truth conditions (the moral authority) of moral judgments may transcend individual moral judgments, neither moral principles drawn up by a particular community nor the judgments upon which they are based are "independent of certain mental states," since they are developed merely out of a consensus of mental states. Moreover, just as a subjective individual moral judgment has no authority to which to appeal except our own "authority" as to what should be the case, similarly a linguistic community that develops its own moral principles merely from a consensus of its own beliefs concerning what it *thinks* is true or right has no justification for those principles except its own authority. In other words, a community's moral code has no standing independent of that society's requiring adherence to it since the code embodies merely that which the community thinks should be adhered to. To put the point in Wittgensteinian terms, it would be "[a]s if someone were to buy several copies of the morning paper to assure himself that what it said was true."[45] From the perspective of moral realism, moral facts are "facts" just because they have authority independent of the mental states or beliefs of particular persons *or* communities. Therefore one cannot make a case for even a modified form of moral realism from a conventionalist perspective, because one cannot even make the case that moral judgments are independent of mental states. A community, by itself, is in no better position than an individual to create an authority for its moral justifications. A Community View, then, at least in its most radical formulation, leads to moral subjectivism as well as epistemological antirealism.[46]

VI

It is not patently evident that Wittgenstein held a Community View of language. Nevertheless, the discussion of Community Views of language and their versions of the private language arguments allows one to arrive at some tentative conclusions. A Community View of language has much to be commended as a theory about language learning and language conventions. In fact our languages are by and large community based, and in fact in all probability neither of the Crusoes could develop a language. Robinson lacks a socialization process and early interaction with other persons that, many argue, empirically are necessary for individual language development.[47] As I shall argue in Chapter 8, Community Views highlight an important Wittgensteinian contribution to philosophy that while nonlinguistic beings have sensations, feel pains, and so on, no human being even knows what her private experiences are or how to distinguish one from another until she has learned a language. What is meant is that, although I have pains, I feel them, and I may even signal their existence through my behavior, I do not understand what they are, how to make sense of them, or how to sort them out from other of my experiences until I have the conceptual tools provided by language to make them distinct. For without the latter I have no notion of "how" at all. Moreover, the diversity and richness of languages are accounted for in part by the diversity of human communities. And consensus, habit, and conventions play central roles in how language evolves and how truth is conceived.

Human beings share practices. Some of these are based on shared reactions as beings of the same species. Others are linguistic practices through which we mediate and interpret the world. Shared linguistic practices entail a community bound together "not by a match in mere externals (facts accessible to just anyone), but a capacity for a meeting of minds."[48] I would argue, however, that these dispositions, reactions, and internally and externally shared practices are not the "bedrock." They do not determine *truths* about the world because we attempt to understand truths through these practices and because we interpret and evaluate these practices themselves. That is, to reiterate some of the points made earlier, we distinguish between rules and rule-following. We do this not only because of shared species reactions, but also because of the notions of sameness, difference, and consistency which, as I shall argue in Chapter 7, are the "bedrock" of our structuring practices, of our development and evaluation of consensus, and of our interpretations of rules through applications.

Therefore one does not have to commit Wittgenstein to epistemological antirealism even while acknowledging a communitarian flavor in his position. This is because Wittgenstein's rejection of idiolectic ratification-independent truths does not entail a conventionalist antirealist position where one simply follows communitarian habits "blindly." The latter commits Wittgenstein to the questionable thesis that all rule-following is interpretation where "for the community itself there is no authority, so no standard to meet."[49] If the notion of a rule allows one to evaluate rule-following as Wittgenstein suggests in §201, one need not assimilate Wittgenstein's views to an antirealist conventionalism. One can question an idiolectic starting place for epistemology and deny the logical privacy of rules and rule-following without adopting an antirealist point of view. This does not imply that Wittgenstein is not an antirealist either, but rather that neither realism nor antirealism is foremost in his philosophical thinking or easily derived from his writings. Neither his attack on idiolectic epistemology nor the private language arguments lead necessarily to antirealism, and such terms may not even be appropriate to the discussion.

There are other intractable problems with a Community View of language as the final word on the topic. The communitarian argues that rules and rule-following develop only in a community through its practices, customs, and habits. The language rules one uses and the conventions one develops, whether they are dispositions or normative standards, are the basis for all language, all thought, and all judgments. They are "forms of life" beyond which we may go no further. This view results in a consensus view of language so that "if everyone agrees upon a certain answer, then no one will feel justified in calling the answer wrong."[50] Thus one cannot evaluate rules of a community or investigate the meta-question of what rules are; one "just goes." According to a Community View the community is the "court of last appeal." Rules are "social dispositions" or social norms through which we make judgments and applications in particular contexts. According to this view, basic rules are not truly standards of correctness because at this level we would not know what it would be to be incorrect. A community can misapply its rules, but it cannot be mistaken about what correctness is, according to this theory. Even if rules are set up as normative standards, one cannot evaluate the standards themselves, or worse, the notion of a rule. They just are, period. But this theory is incomplete. Rules do function as normative standards, we do study them (we have just been doing so), and we analyze and evaluate even such basic concepts as "sameness," consistency," and "correctness."[51]

If rules function merely as community precedent and even indeterminately so, this commits Wittgenstein to the proposition that "no 'truth conditions' or 'corresponding facts' in the world exist."[52] The community norms that set conditions for the use of words are themselves indeterminate. What we call "true" and "false" are assertions of what the community has agreed will be uses of these expressions. Now there is a sense in which this position is a correct one. We cannot escape language. All our ideas are funneled through a particular grammar by which we organize and order our experiences. But this does not necessarily entail the conclusion that language is based *only* on community agreement. It is only when one couples a Community View with the reading of Wittgenstein as an antirealist skeptic that this thesis becomes a plausible alternative. Wittgenstein does not deny the existence of a world independent of our language about which we can make true or false statements. Whether or not what we know about the world is independent of our language is, at best, doubtful, but this need not lead to the questionable conclusion that so-called true or false statements about that world are merely conventional views constructed by a community, albeit a community of human beings.[53] Similarly, moral judgments occur only in social settings. But that fact does not imply that what we take to be moral truths are merely a matter of consensus or community agreement.

The Community View commits us to too much. A consensus-based theory of language, language rules, and language development appears plausible, but it is too restrictive. It is not that we do not agree about linguistic usage, and one need not dispute the thesis that language usually develops in a social context partly out of custom and habit. It is that this is not the whole story. This is because at the base of community agreement (and disagreement) are the notions of consistency, sameness, and difference, notions functioning as the ground for the possibility of disagreement and agreement. These concepts allow consensus *and* change to occur. The idea of a "form of life," if it is to make sense at all, is best applied to these concepts since without them we simply would not function except totally indeterminately and randomly and therefore inexplicably even to ourselves. These are notions about which one cannot dispute, although we have an idea of what it would be like not to have them.

Finally, one of the aims of Community Views is to show that a private language is impossible. But these theses do not solve the private language problem. There are at least two reasons why this is so. First, if a community can develop a language merely on the basis of dispositions or consensus, so too can Robinson Crusoe. So Community Views do not preclude language development in isolation. Conversely, given the presuppositions of a Community View, if the communitarian argues that a person in isolation cannot develop a language, then the communitarian has difficulty showing how a social context provides something isolation lacks.

Second, if rules and rule-following are based on consensus, these are the "bedrock." Accordingly, there is no reason why different communities could not develop social practices (and therefore languages) so different that they would not be comprehensible or translatable to one another. Or, if I translate another language, the translations I made would be from my own community's perspective so that I could never really know or understand the language of another community. Thus the Community Views allow the possibility for a multitude of incommensurable languages, that is, language comprehensible only to a certain community of speakers.

What is wrong with this conclusion? Wittgenstein sometimes talks as if there are some forms of life or ways of dealing with the world that are incommensurable with others. For example, Wittgenstein says, "[i]f a lion could talk, we could not understand him."[54] (More will be said about forms of life in Chapter 6.) So, then, it would be possible that different communities have their own way of dealing with the world that is utterly different from others, thereby each having a distinct language. However, the possibility of incommensurable languages brings into question the private language arguments, since such languages could be incomprehensible to each other and thus private. Now Wittgenstein clearly argues against the possibility of a private language on the micro level, that is, within a community of speakers with whom he is familiar. He does not explicitly consider the possibility of private sets of languages on the macro level even though sometimes his notion of a form of life implies that this could be the case. Yet it would be inconsistent to conclude that a private language is impossible and at the same time admit that there could be languages that are incomprehensible to each other. Yet Community Views allow for just such a conclusion. So either the private language arguments are invalid or the notion of an incommensurable language is impossible. In any event, the Community Views have not shown that a private language is impossible on either the micro or macro level. It remains the task for Chapter 7 to make such an argument.

It might be the case that communitarians have in mind a world-community of human beings or the universal community of *Homo sapiens* as the "bedrock" for agreement. This solution solves the private language problem, at least for *Homo sapiens*.[55] But this still leaves the questionable difficulty of assuming that a world community consensus is the bedrock or a form of life, an assumption we shall challenge in the next chapter.

I conclude that while one cannot learn merely from one's own case by ostensive definition without the notion of a rule (an argument defended in Chapter 3), this conclusion does not lead necessarily either to a denial of truth conditons for language or to an affirmation of a Community View. I accept the *de facto* Community View that most likely we learn language in and from a community and that certain agreements set up conventions for grammar and the uses of words. But, as I shall argue in detail in Chapter 7, the notion of a rule is such that a private language is impossible. Rules are not identical with their applications. The distinction between rules and rule-following explains the generation of new rules, the setting aside and questioning of present ones, and the ways in which we use rules as standards for reevaluation. Moreover, the notion of a rule provides a stability in our understanding that is allegedly lacking in a Wittgensteinian approach to rule-following and allows the evaluation, revision, and even rejection of community practice and consensus. The community, then, is not the court of last appeal. The notion of a rule allows us to stand in judgment of that court.

Notes

1. Peacocke, Reply [to Gordon Baker]: Rule Following: The Nature of Wittgenstein's Arguments," p. 73.
2. Interestingly, in one of his last articles Norman Malcolm espoused this view. See "Wittgenstein on Language and Rules," *Philosophy*, 64 (1989): 5–28.
3. Kripke, *Wittgenstein on Rules and Private Language*, p. 96.
4. Wittgenstein, *PI*, §199.

5. Ibid., §202.
6. Ibid.
7. See, for example, §140 and §149.
8. Wittgenstein, *PI*, §219.
9. Ibid., §217.
10. Anthony Manser, "Pain and Private Language," *Studies in the Philosophy of Wittgenstein*, ed. Peter Winch (London: Routledge & Kegan Paul, 1969), p. 168. Manser's own position on linguistic isolation is confusing. The subject of his reference is Ayer's Robinson Crusoe, a person in physical isolation, so Manser appears to conflate physical isolation with linguistic isolation.
11. For a defense of this thesis see Benjamin F. Armstrong, Jr., "Wittgenstein on Private Languages: It Takes Two to Talk," *Philosophical Investigations* 7 (1984): 46–62.
12. Wittgenstein, *PI*, §265.
13. Armstrong, "Wittgenstein on Private Languages," p. 60.
14. See also Robert Kimball, "Private Criteria and the Private Language Argument," *Southern Journal of Philosophy* 18 (1980): 411–416.
15. See Cora Diamond, "Realism and the Realistic Spirit," in *Ludwig Wittgenstein: Critical Assessments: Volume Four: From World to Sociology: Wittgenstein's Impact on Contemporary Thought*, ed. Stuart Shanker (London: Croom Helm, 1986), pp. 214–242. Diamond suggests that in general Community Views require a form of verification that what one is doing corresponds with community practices or agreed-upon patterns of behavior.
16. Simon Blackburn, "The Individual Strikes Back," *Synthese* 58 (1984): 299. See also Swoyer, "Private Languages and Skepticism," pp. 41–50.
17. See Peacocke, "Reply," pp. 73–75. See also Malcolm, "Wittgenstein on Language and Rules," pp. 5–28.
18. Peacocke, "Reply," p. 73.
19. Wittgenstein, *PI*, §202.
20. Peacocke, "Reply," pp. 73–76.
21. George Pitcher, "About the Same," in *Ludwig Wittgenstein: Philosophy and Language*, ed. Alice Ambrose and Morris Lazerowitz (London: Routledge & Kegan Paul, 1972), pp. 120–139.
22. See Kripke, *Wittgenstein on Rules and Private Language*, pp. 37, 111–112, and the "Introductory Essay" in Holtzman and Leich, pp. 1–30.
23. See Blackburn, "The Individual Strikes Back," pp. 281–302. Paul Hoffman makes a somewhat similar point in a different context. See Paul Hoffman, "Kripke on Private Language," *Philosophical Studies* 47 (1985): 23–28.
24. See Blackburn, "The Individual Strikes Back," pp. 297–300.
25. For a strong defense of this view, see Hintikka and Hintikka, *Investigating Wittgenstein*, Chapter 8. See also Baker and Hacker, *Scepticism, Rules and Language*, pp. 64–81, and McGinn, *Wittgenstein on Meaning*, pp. 78–79. See also Malcolm Budd, "Wittgenstein on Meaning, Interpretation and Rules," *Synthese* 58 (1984): 303–323 for a criticism of this view.
26. Defending a weaker thesis, Robert Fogelin argues that because of the social nature of human beings, *in fact* a private language such as PL$_e$ is contingently

impossible. Fogelin acknowledges that the private language arguments have not established that there is nothing in principle to prevent developing what I have called think-rules and rules by himself. However, Fogelin writes, "[I]n fact, however, human beings are not like this; there are no linguistic self-starters. We thus arrive at the factual conclusion that a necessarily private language is contingently impossible" (*Wittgenstein*, p. 165). What Fogelin is saying is that our (human) nature is such that we are not disposed to develop a language in isolation. This weaker interpretation of the Community Argument, however true empirically, does not affect our conclusion that in principle Robinson could develop a language by himself in isolation.

27. Wittgenstein, *PI*, §84.
28. Crispin Wright, "Rule-Following, Objectivity and the Theory of Meaning," in Holtzman and Leich, p. 102.
29. Ibid., p. 99.
30. Wittgenstein, *PI*, §28.
31. Wright, "Rule-Following," p. 114.
32. Ibid., p. 100; also in Crispin Wright, *Wittgenstein on the Foundations of Mathematics*, p. 216.
33. Wright, "Rule-Following," p. 105.
34. Ibid., p. 114.
35. Ibid., p. 106.
36. Ibid., p. 112.
37. Wittgenstein, *PI*, §225.
38. Ibid., §201.
39. Ibid., Part II, p. 230. As John McDowell writes, ". . . it would be a serious error . . . in his [Wittgenstein's] view, not to make a radical distinction between the significance of, say, 'This is yellow' and the significance of, say, 'This would be called "yellow" by (most) speakers of English.'" John McDowell, "Wittgenstein on Following a Rule," *Synthese* 58 (1984): 335. See also John McDowell, "Non-Cognitivism and Rule-Following," in Holtzman and Leich, pp. 141–162; and G. E. M. Anscombe, "The Question of Linguistic Idealism," p. 189.
40. Sabina Lovibond, *Realism and Imagination in Ethics* (Oxford: Basil Blackwell, 1983), p. 59.
41. Ibid., p. 63.
42. Ibid., p. 81.
43. Walter Sinnott-Armstrong, "Moral Realisms and Moral Dilemmas," *Journal of Philosophy* 84 (1987): 263.
44. Lovibond, p. 71.
45. Wittgenstein, *PI*, §265.
46. See Patricia H. Werhane, "Wittgenstein and Moral Realism," *Journal of Value Inquiry* (1992), forthcoming.
47. See, for example, Suzanne Langer, *Philosophy in a New Key*, especially Chapter 3. Fogelin argues that this is the valid point of the private language arguments. *Wittgenstein*, pp. 165ff.
48. McDowell, "Wittgenstein," p. 351.

49. Wright, *Wittgenstein on the Foundation of Mathematics*, p. 220.
50. Kripke, p. 112.
51. See Baker and Hacker, *Scepticism, Rules and Language*, pp. 64–81.
52. Kripke, p. 86.
53. See Anscombe, pp. 188–215.
54. Wittgenstein, *PI*, Part II, p. 223.
55. See Stephen Davies, "Kripke, Crusoe and Wittgenstein," *Australasian Journal of Philosophy* 66 (1988): 52–66.

5

"This Was Our Paradox"

Community Views of language defend the thesis that "the general practice of the community is constitutive of its linguistic rules."[1] A more radical version of that view takes the position that language evolves out of the brute fact of prelinguistic primitive common agreements in human reactions to the world. These brute agreements form the basis for community and societal consensus out of which rules, rule-following, societal norms, and language evolve. So "general practices" are grounded on primitive consensus or forms of life that are so basic that they are presupposed and implicit in any later formulation of rules, including the norms of truth and falsity, and preclude self-evaluation, since they are the root of the evaluative processes themselves. This thesis, espoused by Saul Kripke in his book, *Wittgenstein: On Rules and Private Language*, is more radical than other Community Views, because it questions the status of conventions and rules themselves as being anything more than assertions based on primitive reactive expressions of agreement. By carrying the notion of conventionalism to a skeptical conclusion, this thesis challenges the grounds of logic and rationality since truth-conditions are merely the assertability conditions of a community. Because of the seriousness of this challenge one must study its arguments carefully both as a way of reading Wittgenstein and as an explanation of language, truth, and the foundation of knowledge.

Deriving his arguments from an examination of the *Philosophical Investigations*, Kripke takes as the pivotal section of that text §201: "This was our paradox: no course of action could be determined by a rule, because every course of action can be made out to accord with the rule." The paradox, according to Kripke, is that one can never know merely from one's past applications or interpretations of a rule whether one is applying the rule correctly in a new instance. This is because one has only a finite set of past uses and indeed, only memories of these, to which to appeal in determining whether the present use accords with the rule in

question. The skeptical paradox has two challenges from this perspective. I must show how I am justified in using a particular rule, for
example, the rule for addition, where my only justification is merely a
finite number of past applications (particular additions). So, first (a) I
must demonstrate the validity of a rule and the correctness (or incorrectness) of interpretations of a rule merely from a finite set of applications.
(b) I must show that what I mean in this particular case, say, by
addition, is the same as what I had meant in doing my last addition
problem. Second, I must be able to justify the alleged fact that $2 + 2 = 4$,
or, in Crispin Wright's terms, I must be able to show the "investigation-
independent" truth of that fact apart from my particular addition.[2] Since
none of these challenges can be met, according to Kripke's reading of
Wittgenstein, Kripke attributes to Wittgenstein a radical rule skepticism
about the objectivity of rules and thus the meanings of words and the
existence of language as well as a skepticism about the truth conditions
underlying our alleged facts about the world. Kripke then contends that
Wittgenstein solves this skeptical paradox because "Wittgenstein proposes a picture of language based, not on *truth conditions*, but on *assertability conditions* or *justification conditions*,"[3] the latter being based on the
"brute fact that we generally agree."[4] This is a version of a Community
View because it denies investigation-independent truths, and because,
Kripke argues, the game of language "would lose its point outside a
community that generally agrees in its practices."[5] There are also differences between Kripke's interpretation of Wittgenstein and those we
analyzed in Chapter 4, as we shall see.

Kripke's reading of the project of the *Philosophical Investigations* raises a
number of issues. These include his evaluation of the notion of a rule,
his interpretation of the private language arguments, his uses of the
term "intention," and his truncated reading of §201. In this chapter I
shall address and attack this interpretation of Wittgenstein as a questionable reading of the *Philosophical Investigations*, and I shall suggest
some alternative interpretations of Wittgenstein's views. Such an attack
is crucial not merely to set the record straight on what Wittgenstein was
about in the *PI*. An acceptance of Kripke's analysis results in a radical
skepticism about rules themselves and thus challenges the rational basis
for truth and language.

I

Like Hume's skeptical analysis of causation, Kripke appears to set up
Wittgenstein's skeptical paradox from a subjective perspective. Indeed,

Kripke argues, there are striking parallels between Hume's and Wittgenstein's skeptical approach. Starting from my intentions to use a rule, such as, the rule for addition, Kripke asserts that I can never justify my present use of a rule (addition) from past uses, since I have no way to judge that the present addition coincides with past uses of that rule except from present use and memories of past uses. Beginning with my own present use of a rule, there are no criteria independent of my present and past intentions and applications of rules to which to appeal to see whether or not I am applying the rule correctly. Moreover, there are no independent facts to evaluate the truth or falsity of whatever conclusions I derive from using a rule, or if there are, I cannot get at them except from my subjective perspective. All I have for evidence of their truth or falsity are the conclusions I have reached previously after a finite number of rule-following practices. If the only criteria for a correct application of a rule or a correct reference of a word are past applications, in trying to determine, for example, whether $2 + 2 = 4$, I am never sure that "+" has the same meaning as in its last instance of use or that 2 is the same as "2" when last referred to. I cannot know whether declarative sentences, for example, correspond to facts, because I cannot establish anything from my own case. One can neither establish any rules or truth conditions independent of my present and past intentions, nor evaluate an application of a rule (e.g., addition) if the only criteria are past applications. So I have no reason, no good objective reason, to assume that $2 + 2 = 4$ is a truth that holds for all possible uses of "plus" or that I have consistently used "plus" as addition. The paradox is that because we can never be sure that our past intentions coincide with our present ones, we can never know whether or not we are applying a rule correctly (or, worse, whether we are even using the same rule again), and we cannot establish criteria for correctness or truth. This argument, then, not only mitigates against the objectivity of rules; it is skeptical about their existence and consistency in application as well.

This seemingly negative conclusion need not lead to absolute nihilism or solipsism. Instead, Kripke argues on behalf of Wittgenstein, we reconstruct this apparently hopeless epistemological situation by shifting the emphasis from examining the connection between words or sentences and facts (a fruitless enterprise)[6] to seeing how words are used and the role language-games play in our practices. Word use is determined not by what is true (since that cannot be determined), but by what a linguistic community *asserts* to be true, or the way that truth is to be understood by that community. As a result, according to Kripke, "we can say that Wittgenstein proposes a picture of language based, not on *truth conditions*, but on *assertability conditions* or *justification conditions.*"

To give a specific example, according to Kripke, it is not the case that we agree that $2 + 2 = 4$ because there is an objective concept of addition that we all understand, or because $2 + 2 = 4$ is true in all possible worlds. Rather, according to this view of the later Wittgenstein, because "[i]n fact our actual community is (roughly) uniform in its practices with respect to addition,"[7] we have identical responses to this arithmetic equation. Kripke, however, does not hold a Dispositional Community View. In fact, Kripke attacks that view at length and argues that "[t]he relation of meaning and intention to future action is *normative*, not *descriptive.*"[8] Language rules, then, are communal norms for how one should go on rather than merely descriptive of communal dispositions. Moreover, according to Kripke, Wittgenstein's position is not that we are following a rule correctly if it agrees with the way most people in a community follow that rule. What we mean by addition, for example, is not merely the definition given that function by most members of our community. For if this were the case, then one could verify whether one was using addition correctly by checking with the community's practice, a conclusion which, Kripke points out, is at odds with Wittgenstein's statement, "Certainly the propositions, 'Human beings believe that twice two is four' and 'Twice two is four' do not mean the same."[9] Such a Community View, what has been labeled a "majoritarian view," introduces truth-conditions for the verification of correctness—the condition being what most of the community accepts as true or correct. Rather, Kripke contends, it is the "brute fact that we generally agree" that is the basis for our assertions. Because we generally agree, in what I would call a "natural consensus," we share common concepts. So we can develop rules for addition that appear to be unquestionable because they are asserted from this brute consensus. It is only when one says, for example, "$2 + 2 = 5$" that we question her judgment. So

> [it] is *not* that the answer everyone gives to an addition problem is, by definition, the correct one, but rather the platitude that, if everyone agrees upon a certain answer, then no one will feel justified in calling the answer wrong.[10]

Kripke's account thus allows for differences between what one does in allegedly following a rule as opposed to what one should do. This enables us to distinguish between thinking we are following a rule and actually doing so, the former occurring when I intend to follow a rule, and the latter being confirmed when my rule-following activities conform to community norms, norms that are part of the way in which a community deals with the world, its "form of life."

This model, Kripke asserts, and thus our language and our views about language, "the set of responses in which we agree . . . is our *form of life*"[11] or the bedrock of our activities, including language, through which we operate and beyond which we cannot penetrate. Therefore a community cannot evaluate its own assertability conditions or its norms for rule-following, nor can it circumvent its own linguistic rule model, since what it asserts is a basic agreed-upon "given."

Kripke uses his version of a Community View of language to attack the notion of a private language, in particular, PL_e, a language developed by one person in social or linguistic isolation. Because language and the justification for word usage depend on rules, rules that develop out of "the brute fact that we generally agree," and which make no sense except as part of the interactions with a community, the notion of a private rule used by an individual in isolation "can have *no* substantive content."[12] A person considered in linguistic isolation, Susan Crusoe, lacks this "brute fact." Susan's only appeal is to her own intentions and fallible memories of past intentions. So anything she does is "all right."

> What is really denied is what might be called the "private model" of rule following, that the notion of a person following a given rule is to be analyzed simply in terms of facts about the rule follower and the rule follower alone, without reference to his membership in a wider community.[13]

Kripke interprets Wittgenstein's statement in §202, "'obeying a rule' is a practice," to mean that one cannot be said to obey a rule in isolation since the conditions for justification for sorting out correct and incorrect applications of a rule are missing. Notice, however, that these conditions are missing in any circumstance, according to Kripke's skeptical position. One is always "locked into one's intentions" so that according to this view one can never establish independent truth-conditions for any alleged fact. Kripke's arguments, then, do not merely mitigate against a contingently private language, that is, a language developed by a solitary individual, but also against any language that tries to establish truth conditions for words and expressions.

Kripke says further that

> The falsity of the private model need not mean that a *physically isolated* individual cannot be said to follow rules; rather that an individual,

considered in isolation (whether or not he is physically isolated), cannot be said to do so.[14]

Robinson Crusoe, in physical isolation, might be said to be able to develop and follow rules, but we can say that because if we stumbled upon him, we would simply transpose our own language rules onto Crusoe's "language." In other words, we would "translate" Crusoeish into English *as if* it followed rules similar to ours, whether it really did or not. According to this view, it is not *the* notion of a rule that disallows the privacy of Crusoe's language but rather our own parochial notion of a rule about which we cannot not agree. It follows that "an individual, considered in isolation" (as opposed to a physically isolated individual) is not merely a person who is out of contact with a community but is also someone with whom one cannot make contact in principle because our notion of a rule simply cannot apply to whatever it is this person does or utters.

Moreover, according to Kripke, one cannot establish truth conditions from one's intentions because one has no independent criteria to establish whether one's past use of a rule such as "plus" is the same as one's present one. So one can never check whether $2 + 2 = 4$ means the same in all instances of application of the sign $+$. Thus Susan by herself could not establish the truth of any of her uses of rules or references of words. One needs a community, then, in which there are already basic agreements, in order to establish rules about the use of words. By the same argument, a community, too, cannot establish truth conditions for its assertions. It cannot check the basis for what it takes to be truth or falsity since it cannot get at investigation-independent facts. But as a community we agree on what we will take to be correct uses of words and correct and incorrect applications of sounds to objects. A person in physical isolation might develop a language if he could establish his own assertability conditions. A person in linguistic isolation could not. Therefore, Kripke would contend, we cannot even conceive of Susan's language development in linguistic isolation because as soon as we consider it we either force whatever it is that Susan is doing into our agreed-upon rule model, or we dismiss Susan's performance as non-linguistic. This is because, according to Kripke, our notion of a language rule is formed from natural consensus through which we interpret or reject other apparently similar or different human activities. Accordingly, Wittgenstein's view of language precludes the possibility of a private language either in the sense of a language developed by a person in isolation or in the usual sense of a language that is incomprehensible to persons other than its creator-speaker, since the former cannot be created in the first place, and the latter is precluded by the fact that whatever a person does is either translated into one's own language or excluded as nonlinguistic.

II

Kripke's explanation of a language rule entails the denial of the possibility of Susan Crusoe's language development. In contrast to Kripke, I shall argue that while it is true that Susan cannot learn merely from her own case without the notion of a rule, this does not preclude in principle her language development or more generally lead to a denial of truth-conditions for language or necessarily commit one to a Community View.

Wittgenstein says, "The use of the word 'rule' and the use of the word 'same' are interwoven."[15] That is, the idea of "same" (and the idea of "difference") is the basis for rules and rule-following. This is because in order to apply a rule correctly and consistently one must be able to distinguish the difference between instances when one is following a rule and instances when one is making a mistake. Consistently using a word or an expression according to certain patterns entails that one understands or can understand what would count as an incorrect use of a word and what would count as using that word in the same way on different occasions. For one could not be said to be applying patterns to one's uses of words if one could not consistently follow the pattern in question so that one could distinguish a misuse of a word in relation to the principle (rule) being used.

As we argued in Chapter 4, if Susan Crusoe, for example, can distinguish between instances when she thinks she is following a rule, say, for addition, from other occasions when she thinks she is not adding, Susan is making a distinction, albeit by herself, between thinking she is applying a rule correctly and not doing so. So Susan must have some sense of consistency so that she can judge whether she even thinks she is "going on in the same way" or differently. Suppose that Susan develops a series of think-rule applications. Since Susan can distinguish between thinking she is following a rule and not doing so, she has the basis for distinguishing between think-rules and following a think-rule. There would be no reason why Susan could not set aside some think-rules, the basis of her applications and distinctions, distinct from her particular applications, that could function as "rules" to evaluate her think-rule-following. And if Susan can construct think-rules, she can also set aside some of these in this way to function as "standards." Of course, as we have noticed, Susan can "cheat" and change her think-rules or allow exceptions, but this happens under more communal circumstances as well.

What is interesting is that if Susan can set up her own think-rules with which to evaluate her think-rule-following, she is in the same linguistic position as a community. Even if we grant with Kripke that Susan cannot set up truth-conditions to verify the correctness of her rule-following she can set up private normative standards, her own "objective" think-rules from her own standards of agreement. Or in other terms, if the basis for language is natural consensus, is it not at least in principle possible that Susan could have "within herself" those same criteria (or different criteria) for agreement? And this is exactly what happens in a community, according to Kripke. If rules are not simply reflections of community dispositions and habits, a view Kripke disputes at length, and if rules are normative standards created by or evolving from the brute fact of our agreement or natural consensus with no verifiable justifications, then there is no reason, no good reason, why Susan in isolation cannot set up similar independent standards by herself as well. Susan, of course, cannot correct her basic notion of "correctness," but neither can a community.

Kripke might not take the foregoing as a counter-argument to his analysis. He might argue that a person in *linguistic* isolation is a person who has *no* concept of a rule whatsoever. In that case Susan could not develop a language. I would agree. Yet Kripke often talks as if it is the case that a person in linguistic isolation has merely her own notion of a rule so that she has no *objective* criteria with which to evaluate this notion. But this is exactly the same position in which a community finds itself. My point is that the notion of a rule does not necessarily depend on a community. Thus if Susan in isolation thinks she has a notion of a rule and can apply it consistently, distinguishing these applications from errors, it is at least theoretically possible that Susan can develop a language without reference to a community. It is on this theoretical point that Kripke and I disagree. Conversely, if we grant that a community in isolation from investigation-independent facts can develop a language, there is no reason not to admit that Susan can develop a language too.

III

There is another difficulty with Kripke's solution to the alleged Wittgensteinian skeptical paradox. Because language is based on a form of life, languages of different communities on this planet could be sufficiently distinct so that the language of one community could in principle be incomprehensible to another community. It follows that if we are visited by beings from another galaxy it might be the case that there would be a total lack of communication because of a different form of life on that galaxy. Moreover, one would never know whether we are communicating or not, because if such aliens came we either could not understand them at all or could only understand them through our consensus-based linguistic forms through which we would translate their utterances or signs into our language. Kripke's interpretation of Wittgenstein, then, like the Community Views we discussed in Chapter 4, has a "private language problem" on the macro level. Because rule-following is a social convention in which we are inexorably intertwined, and since I cannot get a perspective on my own community's point of view because the very concepts and mechanisms that I use to get at that perspective are derived solely from community agreements, I can never evaluate the conventions of aliens except from my own perspective. Therefore, I can never even know whether I understand alien language since my understanding is always a projection of my own community's conventions. I am not sure in fact that Kripke means to hold this view or attributes it to Wittgenstein. But his interpretation of language development and rule-following allows no mechanism to explain why such incomprehensibility between two languages could not at least in principle occur. So Kripke's reading of Wittgenstein, developed in part to argue against the possibility of a private language, creates its own private language problem on another level.

Kripke gets caught with a private language problem at least in part because of the alleged identification of communal brute agreements as forms of life. This identification precludes communal self-evaluation of its agreements and thus precludes the evaluation of other communities except through one's own perspective. However, this is too narrow a view. Community agreements, I would argue, are not the bedrock of language. One can evaluate, revise, and even reject community standards, responses, and even natural consensus.[16] It is true that one cannot imagine a community in which there were no basic agreements. But it is not merely that as a community or as human beings we intuitively sense "how to go on" and "how to go on correctly" so that what is correct is an assertion deriving from this intuitive sense or agreement. Underlying that are more basic distinctions that allow us to go on at all and thus underpin natural consensus. To use a passage from the *Philosophical Investigations* to support this,

> If anyone believes that certain concepts are absolutely the right ones, and that having different ones would mean not realizing something that we realize—then let him imagine certain very general facts of nature to be different from what we are used to, and the formation of concepts different from usual ones will become intelligible to him.[17]

The notion of a rule, the idea of the sameness of response, allows us to form concepts and develop basic agreements and thus even evaluate and change them.

It is in this latter sense that rules are normative. Because of the normative and evaluative character of rules, addition, for example, is a convention upon which we agree, but it is more than that as well. It is one of a series of formal applications consistently applied to a certain kind of relationship between objects. Addition is also a rule we use to cut across conventions. We study addition as a rule to see whether and how well it applies consistently and universally to relationships between numbers and numbered phenomena with which we come into contact.

Kripke's interpretation of Wittgenstein could be attributed to his narrow reading of what Wittgenstein means by the term "private." The term "private" can be taken in at least three ways: (1) as referring to phenomena that are experienced or knowable only to one person, in contrast to public objects; (2) as talking about what is understood only to one person, in contrast to what is translatable or publicly comprehensible; and (3) as referring to individuals or individual practices in contrast to group or social practices. Sometimes Kripke appears to treat "private" to mean merely (3) the individual as opposed to the social perspective. Thus when Wittgenstein chastises the notion of private rule-following in §199 and §202, Kripke misinterprets this to be a questioning of isolated individual rule-following. This leads Kripke to use §199 as an argument in support of obeying a rule as a *social* (as opposed to an isolated) practice. But if the term "private" is taken in the sense of (1) or (2), rule-following *can* be individual.[18] I take §199 to mean merely that rules are neither "things" nor unique, one-occurrence phenomena. Rather, rules are formal mechanisms that set out guidelines for a number of varied and repeatable applications or interpretations. In any event,

Kripke's view appears to restrict rules to *social* practices (in his sense of "social," which is, at best, probably not what Wittgenstein means in every case), and this also restricts the definition of a private language to refer merely to a language that one develops in isolation rather than to a language (wherever or however it is developed) that is incomprehensible to others.

Perhaps, however, we have not carefully interpreted Kripke's point as an attack on the private model of rule-following. It may be the case that Kripke interprets Wittgenstein as attacking a private model of rule-following wherein we grasp determinate pictures, formulas, or rules "in our mind" and then justify the uses of words or applications of rules or formulas from this mental picture or intuitive grasp.[19] "'It is as if we could grasp the whole use of the word in a flash.'"[20] If such an association of a mental picture or formula is an ostensive one, it cannot determine future uses of applications of that picture or formula. This is because any such association entails a rule for linking like associations, a rule that is not part of the ostensive associative process. Such a rule is missing in ostensive associations so that when I attempt to reapply the rule or picture I cannot ascertain whether I am making the same rule-application association or merely think I am.

Wittgenstein's attack here is on the model of private mental ostensive association. But this does not altogether preclude that Susan in isolation could not make such associations. For if a person in isolation could understand the notion of "sameness of response" (and difference) and apply these notions consistently, she could grasp the rule underlying ostensive rule associations and thereby repeat the associations and correct her errors. Attacking the private "mental" ostensive model of rule-following does not entail a commitment to the community or "social" model.[21] For the latter view entails a rejection of the "solitary" model of rule-following while the former entails a rejection of private ostensive association as the basis for rules and rule-following. These are obviously distinct. Yet Kripke insists that Wittgenstein rejects a "mental ostensive model" while solving the skeptical paradox with a form of a Community View of language, and it is this latter conclusion that is being questioned here.

Kripke's denial of the "private model" of rule-following is puzzling. Kripke asserts that assertability conditions are community based. When I say, "2 + 2 = 4 is true," I am saying that my particular addition agrees with the community norm in regard to addition. Each time I add, I at least implicitly compare my addition to this norm and judge its correctness or incorrectness accordingly. The norm, then, is the criterion, the "type," of which my particular addition is a "token." The assertability conditions for my saying "2 + 2 = 4" are therefore descriptive of addition norms exemplified by the relationship between my additions and community norms; they say nothing about the world or about meaning.

But why is it not possible for an individual in isolation, say Susan Crusoe, to set up her own "type" to which she responds with particular applications, some of which are correct and some of which, influenced by her changing whims or inclinations, are not? Susan's assertability conditions would then be descriptive of her practices made in relation to the type she had set up.[22] Kripke claims that assertability conditions for correctness depend on responses that correlate my additions with the rule for addition prescribed by community agreements. Any such token-type relationship (or in my terms, the relationship between applications of a rule or rule-following practices and a rule) assumes an agreement between tokens and type. But if "[t]he notion of agreement rests on the notion of sameness of response" which in turn "requires knowledge of the correct continuations according to a rule,"[23] isolated Susan's practices could meet this criterion, if she knows how to go on in the same way according to the type or rule she has set up for herself. So Kripke's argument that a solitary language is impossible fails from this point of view.

Furthermore, it is not clear that a community or an individual could have "knowledge of the correct continuations according to a rule" in Kripke's skeptical scheme, because Kripke talks as if assertability conditions obtain merely from an agreement between my applications of a rule and community norms. Thus "sameness of response" is measured in terms of the relationship between my use of addition and the community's brute agreements. Each time I add I must make this comparison rather than gaining any personal knowledge about whether or not I am going on in the same way since according to Kripke I cannot know, merely from my own intentions, whether or not I have succeeded in adding even when I have performed additions thousands of times.

IV

Kripke generates his explication of rule-following, of course, to solve the skeptical paradox he attributes to Wittgenstein. And herein lies the most serious difficulty with Kripke's interpretation: the way in which

Kripke sets up the paradox that produces a questionable reading of Wittgenstein's notion of rule-following and a realist description of "intention." The basis for his skeptical interpretation of the *Philosophical Investigations* derives from his analysis of the first sentence of §201. But quoted fully, this paragraph says,

> This was our paradox: no course of action could be determined by a rule, because every course of action can be made out to accord with the rule. The answer was: if everything can be made out to accord with the rule, then it can also be made out to conflict with it. And so there would be neither accord nor conflict here.
>
> It can be seen that there is a misunderstanding here from the mere fact that in the course of our argument we give one interpretation after another; as if each one contented us at least for a moment, until we thought of yet another standing behind it. What this shews is that there is a way of grasping a rule which is *not* an *interpretation*, but which is exhibited in what we call "obeying the rule" and "going against it" in actual cases.
>
> Hence there is an inclination to say: every action according to the rule is an interpretation. But we ought to restrict the term "interpretation" to the substitution of one expression of the rule for another.

Kripke's failure to take into account §201 as a whole distorts his version of Wittgenstein's position.[24] In the second part of §201 Wittgenstein argues that *not* every action is an interpretation of a rule (an application) since, in addition to using rules we can distinguish between "'what we call obeying a rule' and 'going against it' in actual cases." Even if every application of a rule is an interpretation, "there is a way of grasping a rule which is *not* an *interpretation*." So there is a rule, or a way of "grasping a rule," the source of applications, that is itself not an application or an interpretation.

In §201 taken as a whole it is plausible that Wittgenstein is distinguishing rules or "grasping a rule" (understanding a rule) from rule-following. Yet one must take care here not to read too much into this passage. Taking the instance of 2 + 2 = 4, can Wittgenstein be interpreted as saying that there is a rule for "plus" in addition to its application? Well, yes and no. One may not be able to isolate the formal principle, "plus," yet be capable of doing complex additions. In applying a rule (doing complex additions) one is in a sense grasping it without consciously doing so. But this does not necessarily commit one to a Kripkean interpretation of addition. For at the same time Wittgenstein recognizes that we operate *as if* there was a rule of which adding

2 + 2 is an application, because we can evaluate each application. Kripke's Community View explains the fact that we both add and evaluate our use of the rule for addition by suggesting that the community's norms for rule-following are just those in which there is basic agreement. These norms themselves are natural directives as to how rule-following should go on. But one could also read Wittgenstein as saying that there are preconditions for rule-following that underlie addition and are not derived merely from natural consensus since they are the grounds for the brute fact of agreement that sets up norms for consistent applications of rules in the first place. So one can interpret §201 as Wittgenstein's questioning the very skepticism that Kripke attributes to him.

Kripke appears to destroy this distinction between rule-following and evaluation because natural consensus functions both to establish rules and to develop criteria for acceptable rule-following practices. So one cannot evaluate rule-following practices except by the same criteria or agreements out of which rules evolved in the first place.[25] Not to be able to distinguish rules from rule-following practices creates the further difficulty of not being able to distinguish between thinking I am following a rule and actually doing so, and this certainly is not the sort of conclusion Wittgenstein wanted to draw.

Part of Wittgenstein's alleged paradox centers on the question, "How do my past intentions affect my present ones?" Thus Wittgenstein's alleged antirealism about truth conditions derives from Kripke's erroneous emphasis on intentions as the source of justification for rule-following. Wittgenstein himself focuses on the question, "How does a rule determine its applications?" rather than on "How do my past intentions affect my present ones?" Wittgenstein, then, is not concerned with intention or introspection of one's intentions ("mental states") at all. To elaborate on this latter point, we need to examine the problem of intention and introspection Kripke introduces. In §201 Wittgenstein attacks the interpretation of understanding as an inner process or a mental state. Kripke's failure to emphasize Wittgenstein's argument that understanding is not an inner process may or may not affect Kripke's reading of Wittgenstein as a skeptic. However, Wittgenstein's attack on the notion of understanding as a mental state or an inner process is antithetical to Kripke's position if the attack is extended to include intentions.[26]

In his use of the word "intention" Kripke speaks as if one *begins* merely from one's own intentions. I start performing what I think are additions; then I wonder whether my actions are consistent with my past intentions to add, whether they follow rules, and whether those rules are independent of my particular performances of what I take to be addition. Since I can answer these questions only by referring to my previous intentions I am "stuck" within my own intentions and memories of past uses, just as David Hume, for example, is "stuck" within impressions and memories (ideas). From this perspective what we call a person is a "bundle of intentions." "There can be no such thing as meaning anything by any word. Each new application we make is a leap in the dark; any present intention could be interpreted so as to accord with anything we may choose to do."[27]

This analysis, however, raises a number of questions. First, what does Wittgenstein mean by the term "intention"? Second, do intentions always play the role Kripke thinks they do in rule-following, or is it more propitious to adopt another notion of rules and rule-following? One should distinguish two uses of the term "intention" that might be useful to get at what is at issue in this context. In brief, we use intention to talk about actions, activities we undertake deliberately or with self-conscious forethought, or actions for which we are responsible. "Intention" is also used to refer to mental states such as desires or beliefs.[28] Now Kripke sometimes confuses these two uses of intention, a confusion that may lead him to misread Wittgenstein. In Chapter 2 of *Wittgenstein on Rules and Private Language* Kripke recognizes that Wittgenstein probably does not view understanding as an introspective mental state.[29] Yet in that same chapter he says, "[b]y means of my external symbolic representation and my internal mental representation, I 'grasp' the rule for addition."[30] And later in the next chapter he declares that "[t]he important problem for Wittgenstein is that my present mental state does not appear to determine what I *ought* to do in the future."[31] Since Wittgenstein's paradox has to do with the impossibility of making inferences about rules and rule-following from one's own intentions, Kripke appears to be talking about intentions as if they were mental states.

Kripke admits that this talk of mental states or mental processes may be a result of his own "linguistic intuitions."[32] Wittgenstein himself sometimes seems to talk about intentions as if they were mental states. In §205 he says, "But it is just the queer thing about *intention*, about the mental process, that the existence of a custom, of a technique, is not necessary to it." This passage, however, is in quotations, which is usually an indication that Wittgenstein disagrees with what is quoted. In §653 he criticizes the "mental state" interpretation of intention.

Wittgenstein argues that "[a]n intention is embedded in its situation, in human customs and institutions."[33] More specifically he means that an intention is not a distinct part of any situation or action. It is the action or interpretation.

> The intention *with which* one acts does not "accompany" the action any more than the thought "accompanies" speech. Thought and intention are neither "articulated" nor "non-articulated"; to be compared neither with a single note which sounds during the acting or speaking, nor with a tune.[34]

This notion of intention is particularly important in rule-following. In rule-following I act and I usually act intentionally in accordance with a rule. But I seldom reflect on the rule. This is perhaps what Wittgenstein meant when he said, "[w]hen I obey a rule I do not choose. I obey the rule *blindly*." Intentionality is part of a rule-following action. What is meant is that following a rule is doing something intentionally and the intention both is part of the interpretation of the rule and determines the way in which the rule is to be interpreted. I can correct my action, the way I follow a rule, but I cannot correct my intention, since my intention is now to correct my former rule-following habits, and that latter intention is part of the corrective action I undertake. Therefore, unlike mental states, intentions that function as actions are inseparably part of those actions. This explains the fact that I usually do not reflect on my intention to add—I merely do sums.[35]

According to Kripke's view of intentions as mental states, intentions function as self-reflective mechanisms to determine whether my past intentions of the use of "plus," for example, coincide with my present intention to use "plus" in a certain way. In these situations I am examining my present rule-following practices. The problem is that I cannot determine whether or not I am following a rule or following a rule correctly merely from my past and present rule-following practices. But this explanation is not entirely accurate. If I can introspect and examine these goings-on (my past and present intentional rule-following actions), then surely I can compare these rule-following activities with a rule they supposedly exemplify. In other words, if intention is a mental state, then by introspection I could sort out rule-following intentional mental states from the rule they supposedly exemplify. So even if Wittgenstein thinks that intentions can function as mental states as well as activities, Wittgenstein is not caught in the paradox attributed to him by Kripke. Now it is probably more likely that Wittgenstein does not accept a "mental state interpretation" of intentions. My point is that if his problem is that "my present mental state does not appear to determine what I *ought* to do in the future," Wittgenstein need not be caught up in the paradox attributed to him as a result of being trapped in past and present intentions.

The reason that Wittgenstein is unlikely to hold a "mental state" view of intention is that it is exactly this sort of approach to philosophy that Wittgenstein often attacks in the *Philosophical Investigations*. One of the problems, according to Wittgenstein, is whether "I know . . . only from my own case."[36] If one cannot begin doing philosophy merely from one's own impressions or sensations, so it follows that one cannot analyze one's mental state intentions merely from one's past intentions. The Crusoes, for example, may have impressions and intentions, but they learn what they are only when they develop or learn language. If one cannot begin philosophical analysis merely from one's own intentions, one need not get caught up in the difficulties that Kripke attributes to Wittgenstein. The private language arguments themselves are directed to preclude this sort of paradox. One could not be said to use a rule even once (e.g., the rule for "plus" or "quus") without having at least implicit conceptions of "use" and "misuse." So one cannot begin doing philosophy merely from one's intentions just as one cannot merely from one's own sensations. In other words, in order to develop a skeptical position on the nature of rules, one needs a conceptual apparatus including language, an apparatus that precludes the radically skeptical position of being caught merely in one's own intentions.

Kripke would probably reply that the reason that there appears to be no skeptical paradox is because each of us finds him/herself in a community in which various complex agreements on rules have already been formulated from what is agreed upon. I learn those customs and norms when I learn language. While I can never get at the independent rule for addition or at the truth of $2 + 2 = 4$, I think I can, because I have internalized conventions originating in natural consensus that prescribe how one will relate numbers to each other. This move shifts the burden to brute agreements so that the paradox now is that I cannot get at the basis for that community agreement, the independent grounds for justifying addition as a rule. Or to put Kripke's point another way, we agree on the meaning of "plus." Such agreement cannot develop merely from my own case. Yet one cannot establish the truth of the rule of addition or that $2 + 2 = 4$ in all possible worlds, because one cannot establish "investigation-independent" truth values either on an individual or on a communal level. The brute fact of agreement precludes that 2 + 2 could be other than 4.

Kripke may be assuming (or reading Wittgenstein to assume) that the only way to establish truth-conditions for a statement is individually in an idiolect. Since this is impossible according to Wittgenstein, Kripke rules out other alternatives for establishing truth conditions. But what Wittgenstein is arguing is that one's intentions, the "process of one's consciousness," one's sense data or sensations are not possible *starting places* for anything. Beginning merely from my own case by primitive ostensive definition gets one nowhere. This argument, however, does not preclude objectivity and truth; it merely precludes idiolectic-based investigation-independent truths. Meaning is situated in rule practices, but truth may not be.[37]

V

Finally, let us briefly consider Kripke's antirealist interpretation of the *Philosophical Investigations*. Kripke commits Wittgenstein to a radically conventionalist view of truth such that truth-conditions are replaced by assertability conditions. Because I cannot establish or verify any facts merely by examining my past and present intentions, I can never know whether 2 + 2 = 4 is true. I must merely rely on what a community asserts to be true in using addition. However, if we are not caught up in our own intentions as mental states, and if at the same time there are difficulties with the contention that community agreements are the last word, the bedrock for all our beliefs and thus our language, then one need not commit Wittgenstein to such an antirealist position. Moreover, even if one grants with Kripke that language rules depend on natural consensus so that a person in isolation could not develop a language by herself or establish the truth conditions for declarative statements merely from her own intentions, it does not necessarily follow that all of one's beliefs are only a result of such agreements. Rather, what one needs to show is how a realist position is at least not inconsistent with a nonidiolectic view of language rules and language development. Admittedly, Wittgenstein himself does not take up this task, but there is no reason on that account to commit him to this sort of conventionalist position.

Taking the opposite point of view in response to an antirealist interpretation, some philosophers try to ascribe a form of realism to the later Wittgenstein.[38] I interpret Wittgenstein as saying that the notion of a rule provides the basis for truth conditions. Although these notions are the preconditions and basis for language I would not go so far as to call them "nonlinguistic," because we can only get at these notions through language. Nevertheless, the notion of a rule precludes neither the possibility of truth conditions functioning in language nor the ascription of a form of realism to Wittgenstein. None of these alternatives, however, is clearly Wittgenstein's, because Wittgenstein's aim is what we might call "label-eradication," the discontinuance of philosophical labeling of views, such as calling someone a Realist, an Anti-Realist, an Idealist, and so on. So while there is good reason not to label Wittgenstein as an antirealist there is little in the way of positive evidence to label him a realist or an idealist, and this is what Wittgenstein wanted.

Kripke's interpretation of Wittgenstein as a skeptic, then, belies Wittgenstein's arguments about rules, rule-following, and language. His Community View arrests philosophical analysis, and it is an unnecessary outcome of the private language arguments. His analysis of intention unduly subjectifies Wittgenstein's arguments, while reifying "intention" as a mental state. Many of Wittgenstein's arguments are constructed to attack this very position. Finally, such a thesis does not even solve the "private language problem," since, as we have argued, if a community can develop a language on the basis of consensus or norms, so too can the Crusoes. Both languages are candidates for "private language" from this perspective, since there is no way to understand either of them except to "translate" whatever they utter into our own meanings and uses. On the contrary, as I shall argue at length in Chapter 7, the proper notion of a rule, while allowing solitary linguists, precludes the possibility of a language that is comprehensible only to its speaker, while avoiding some of the questionable points of Kripke's interpretation of Wittgenstein. Such a thesis will be an antidote both to Kripke's radical rule skepticism and to its counterintuitive conclusion that truth-conditions are merely assertability conditions. Thus valid private language arguments do not undermine the possibility of human knowledge in the way in which Kripke's arguments imply.

Notes

1. Temkin, "A Private Language Argument," p. 111.
2. See Wright, "Rule-Following, Objectivity, and the Theory of Meaning," pp. 99ff.
3. Kripke, *Wittgenstein on Rules and Private Language*, p. 74.

4. Ibid., p. 97.
5. Ibid., p. 96.
6. Ibid., p. 72.
7. Ibid., p. 91.
8. Ibid., p. 37.
9. Wittgenstein, *PI*, Part II, p. 226.
10. Kripke, p. 112.
11. Ibid., p. 96.
12. Ibid., p. 89.
13. Ibid., p. 109.
14. Ibid., p. 110.
15. Wittgenstein, *PI*, §225.
16. As Warren Goldfarb argues, "The notion of agreement rests on the notion of sameness of response." Warren Goldfarb, "Kripke on Wittgenstein on Rules," *The Journal of Philosophy* 82 (1985): 483.
17. Wittgenstein, *PI*, Part II, p. 230.
18. See McGinn, *Wittgenstein on Meaning*, pp. 79–81, for this point.
19. Margaret Gilbert, "On the Question Whether Language has a Social Nature: Some Aspects of Winch and Others on Wittgenstein," *Synthese*, 56 (1983): 315–316.
20. Wittgenstein, *PI*, §191.
21. Gilbert, p. 316.
22. Goldfarb, pp. 483ff.
23. Ibid., p. 484.
24. See, for example, McGinn, *Wittgenstein on Meaning*, Chapter 2, and Baker and Hacker, *Scepticism, Rules and Language*, Chapter 1.
25. See Baker and Hacker, *Scepticism, Rules and Language*, pp. 100–122.
26. This issue is nicely summarized by McGinn. He argues that in §201,

> Wittgenstein does *not* say that the paradox arises from the misunderstanding that ascriptions of rules state facts or have truth conditions, nor does he suggest that the underlying mistake is to consider the rule-follower in social isolation; what he is objecting to is the specific conception of understanding as a mental operation of translation. (*Wittgenstein on Meaning*, pp. 68–69)

27. Kripke, *Wittgenstein on Rules and Private Language*, p. 55.
28. Michael Bratman, "Two Faces of Intention," *Philosophical Review* 93 (1984): 375–406.
29. Kripke, *Wittgenstein on Rules and Private Language*, pp. 49–50.
30. Ibid., p. 7.
31. Ibid., p. 56.
32. Ibid., p. 49.
33. Wittgenstein, *PI*, §337.
34. Ibid., *PI*, p. 217. See also §635.
35. See Paul Moser and Kevin Flannery, "Kripke and Wittgenstein: Intention without Paradox," *The Heythrop Journal* 26 (1985): 311–316. See also Oscar

Hanfling, "Was Wittgenstein a Sceptic?" *Philosophical Investigations* 8 (1985): pp. 1–16.

36. Wittgenstein, *PI*, §347.
37. See McDowell, "Wittgenstein on Following a Rule," pp. 342–343, and McGinn, *Wittgenstein on Meaning*, Chapter 1.
38. Baker and Hacker, for example, argue that Wittgenstein's own position on realism is similar to his views on rules and rule-following, that is, that language and reality are internally related just as rules and rule-following are. Focusing on the notion of a language-game, Hintikka and Hintikka claim that far from being an antirealist, in his later writings Wittgenstein sees "the role of language-games as constituting the basic semantical links between language and reality." *Investigating Wittgenstein*, p. 212, emphasis omitted. Other philosophers have argued that one might read into Wittgenstein a "non-linguistic type-token distinction." The assumption is that apart from our linguistic customs, there are "common properties making a plurality of things tokens of a single type, and thereby providing a criterion or sameness" Moser and Flannery, "Kripke and Wittgenstein: Intention without Paradox," p. 318.

6

"Look On the Language-Game as the *Primary* Thing"

An adequate private language argument should preclude the logical privacy of any language and bring into question the possible incommensurability of languages of different communities. In questioning linguistic relativism the theory of language embedded in such arguments should raise doubts about many forms of conventionalism. Such a theory might also make a positive case for a form of realism as well. These formidable tasks are the aim of the fresh interpretation of Wittgenstein by Merrill Hintikka and Jaakko Hintikka in their book, *Investigating Wittgenstein*. While I shall raise some questions about their analysis, Hintikka and Hintikka challenge us to think carefully about language rules and language-games, they reformulate the relationship between language and reality, and they invite us to examine carefully the implications of Wittgenstein's expression, "form of life." The discussion of their thought will be fruitful, then, as an antidote to Community Views and to help us draw some tentative conclusions about the relationship between language and reality, the roles of rules, and the notion of a form of life.

I

Responding to the Community Views and to what the authors call the "received view," and in reaction to the argument that the notion of a rule is constitutive of language and language development, a view suggested in the last two chapters and one I shall develop in the next, Hintikka and Hintikka have proposed what I shall call the Language-Game Thesis. This thesis argues, in brief,

115

(1) "[l]anguage-games [are] the basic semantical links between language and reality."[1]
(2) "Language-games are truly the measure of all things,"[2] i.e., language-games are the "bedrock" or form(s) of life underlying all human activities.

It follows from these two conclusions that

(3) Language-games are the grounds for, and constitutive of, rules, rule-following, community agreements, and social practices.

The term "language-game" is both important and confusing in Wittgensteinian literature. Sometimes in the *Philosophical Investigations* Wittgenstein uses this expression to talk about primitive languages or simple language-games. "I . . . will sometimes speak of a primitive language as a language-game."[3] More often the expression "language-game" refers to how a word or expression is used in a family of contexts. In discussing ostensive definitions we noticed the importance of the context in which an ostensive association is made to establish the definition in question. The context, the language-game, or the "wider horizon of related rule-governed activities"[4] form the backdrop for the ways in which words are used and rules are followed in particular contexts or situations. Thus, when Wittgenstein says that "following a rule is a practice" he means that rule-following occurs in a context, the context of a complex or nexus of rules functioning in a language-game: "Think how we learn to use the expressions 'Now I know how to go on,' 'Now I can go on' and others; in what family of language-games we learn their use."[5]

The notion of a language-game is also useful to explain Wittgenstein's famous remark, "For a *large* class of cases—though not for all—in which we employ the word 'meaning' it can be defined thus: the meaning of a word is its use in the language."[6] It is not merely following a rule that defines a word. It is the use of an expression in the context of a language-game that defines it, regulates its meaning, and accounts for the fact that meanings of words or expressions change without violation of meaning when that word or expression is used in a different language-game. The term "language-game," then, explains both the multiple ways that language functions and the creative or changing nature of language.

And this multiplicity ["of kinds of use of what we call 'symbols,' 'words,' 'sentences'"] is not something fixed, given once for all; but new types of language, new language-games, as we may say, come into existence, and others become obsolete and get forgotten.[7]

Sometimes "language-game" refers to a way of dealing with a topic in which the kind of approach one adopts to the topic or range of concepts affects one's view of the topic or one's conclusions. A language-game could consist of a particular activity or state of mind, such as intending, hoping, pretending, or believing, each of which affects differently the way we experience a phenomenon or an event. Or a language-game could be more encompassing, for example, the language-game of science, or psychology, or even religious belief.

Language-games are also connected with Wittgenstein's concept of a "form of life," although how they are related is unclear. Wittgenstein says, "[T]he term 'language-game' is meant to bring into prominence the fact that the *speaking* of language is part of an activity, or of a form of life,"[8] where "form of life" is defined as "[w]hat has to be accepted, the given."[9] So a language-game or a series of language-games could constitute a form of life.[10] Perhaps the notion of a language-game itself is a form of life. We shall discuss this connection in more detail in Section V.

About language-games Wittgenstein says, "I shall . . . call the whole, consisting of language and the actions into which it is woven, the 'language-game.'"[11] Hintikka and Hintikka interpret this passage as saying that a language-game encompasses nonlinguistic as well as linguistic activities. This implies that every human activity is a language-game, or even that the totality of human activities is itself a language-game or a form of life on a macro scale. It is perhaps more accurate to say that since they are called *language*-games, language-games include all linguistic activities and "mediate" or are the "links" between linguistic and nonlinguistic activities. Language-games place words and expressions of a language in a context and thus give them their meaning through their use in that context. The point is that language-games are not merely verbal or written, they are not merely utterances or expressions, but include the nonlinguistic context in which the utterance or writing is embedded.

It is obvious from our brief discussion that Wittgenstein uses the term "language-game" to refer to a variety of both specific and general activities or practices so that his definition of a language-game is at best not clear-cut. Nevertheless, the notion of a language-game is a unique Wittgensteinian contribution to philosophical analysis. It explains how it is that words and expressions function in contexts, contexts that dictate the uses and meanings of words and expressions, that structure and regulate rule-following activities, yet are flexible enough to account for changes of meaning and the evolution of ideas. The emphasis on the notion of a language-game in the later Wittgenstein, then, is most justified.

II

According to Hintikka and Hintikka, the two most important functions of a language-game thesis are (1)

> . . . to emphasize the role of rule-governed human activities in constituting the basic representative relationships between language and reality, . . . [and (2)] to highlight the fact that language can be used in many different ways, not just descriptively.[12]

The term "language-game" may refer to a particular activity thus pointing to the variety of rule-governed human activities, or to entire language-games, that is, rule-governed activities in general. However, it should be emphasized that according to Hintikka and Hintikka, "[I]t is the idea of a language-game that in Wittgenstein's later philosophy replaces the role of rules.[13] . . . In later Wittgenstein, language-games are truly the measure of all things."[14] The notion of a rule is a relative one, and the ways in which rules function are dependent on the context or language-game in which they operate. In learning language one does not learn rules. "Rather, a student is *trained* to master the language-game."[15] "These language-games are conceptually prior to their rules."[16] Rules, then, are dependent on language-games rather than the reverse.

One could argue that rule-following is not the essence of language-games, because language-games are more primitive. They are part of the "common history" of humankind—the precondition for language and other human activities including all rule-governed activities.[17] Hintikka and Hintikka would say, I think, that while at least some language-games are in some sense primitive because they underlie human activities, their "mode of operation," so to speak, is in a rule-governed way and that "rule-governedness" is what distinguishes human activities from other kinds of activities. We shall see that what Hintikka and Hintikka call "primary language-games" most aptly fit this notion of the "common history" of humankind, although they are careful to emphasize that according to their reading of Wittgenstein, language-games form the semantical link between language and reality, of which "common history" is only a part.

Although much has been made of the second function of language-games in the literature on the later Wittgenstein, that is, "that language can be used in many different ways," Hintikka and Hintikka emphasize that the first function is equally if not more important. According to Hintikka and Hintikka and counter to Wright's and Kripke's interpretation of Wittgenstein, in his later writings Wittgenstein was a physicalist. Far from being an antirealist, Wittgenstein held that "language must be capable of being compared with reality *directly*,"[18] and "it is entire language-games that serve in this all-important mediating role."[19] This is supported by Wittgenstein:

> Now what do the words of this language *signify*?—What is supposed to shew what they signify, if not the kind of use they have? And we have already described that . . .
> Of course, one can reduce the description of the use of the word . . . to the statement that this word signifies this object.[20]

Rather than holding an antirealist position, then, Wittgenstein developed the notion of a language-game as part of his continuing effort, begun in the *Tractatus*, to explain the connection between language and the world. In his later writings, Wittgenstein turns from the phenomenalism of the *Tractatus* to an "everyday" physicalism in the *Investigations*. In this transition Wittgenstein came to believe that the notion of a language-game best explains the relation between language and reality.

According to their reading of the later Wittgenstein, Wittgenstein's abandonment of the phenomenalism of the *Tractatus* involves a questioning of name-object relationships as the most basic and a realization that verification does not explain every kind of meaning. But, counter to the Community Views, Wittgenstein does not abandon all forms of realism. Rather, Wittgenstein sees the complicated relationships between language and reality and accounts for their diversity and complexity through postulating language-games as the "mediating links" between language and the world. Since "the basic semantical links connecting the expressions of our language with the ingredients of our world are no longer one-to-one relations,"[21] language-games, which can connect a variety of expressions with the world, are not all descriptive and therefore can integrate very complex relationships and thus better account for these semantical links.

Similarly, according to Hintikka and Hintikka, Wittgenstein sees the private language arguments as not aimed at denying that we have private experiences but rather at trying to get at how we talk about these experiences. Although Wittgenstein abandoned his phenomenalism or what Hintikka and Hintikka call a phenomenological point of view in his later writing, Hintikka and Hintikka contend that

> . . . in replacing a phenomenological basis language by a physicalistic one Wittgenstein did not want to alter the ontological status of phenomenological objects, including private experiences. The world we live in remained for him a world of phenomenological objects; but we must talk about them in the language we use to talk about physical objects.[22] . . . [T]he world we live in is the world of sense-data.[23]

The purpose of the private language arguments is to argue against the possibility of a phenomenological language and to explain how we talk about sense data in physicalistic language. It is in this context that Wittgenstein allegedly introduces the notion of a physiognomic language-game.

To explain passages in the *Investigations* such as §244, §257, and Part II, xi, p. 207, and to account for our publicly understood talk about and references to private sense experiences, Hintikka and Hintikka argue that Wittgenstein postulates primary language-games.

> On at least one occasion ["Notes for Lectures on 'Private Experience' and 'Sense Data'"], Wittgenstein explicitly makes a distinction between the two kinds of language-games, *viz.*, a distinction between, on the one hand, the language-game which gives a certain word its meaning (and through which we learn this meaning), and, on the other hand, the language-game in which we utter the word.[24]

The former, primary language-games, are by and large what Hintikka and Hintikka call "physiognomic language-games." There are also other primary language-games, for example, physiological language-games, but it will turn out that physiognomic language-games are the most important ones. Physiognomic language-games are primary in the sense that they are semantic manifestations or expressions of phenomena or experiences. Physiognomic language-games that are expressions of private experiences give a public framework for these experiences, an inexorable link between sense experiences and language. According to Wittgenstein, "The language-games with expressions of feelings are based on games with expressions of which we don't say that they may lie."[25] What is distinctive about primary language-games is that they are natural expressions or spontaneous manifestations logically linked to the reality they manifest. Therefore, they are not verifiable, or true or false. They are in that sense incorrigible.

[I]n primary language-games, criteria and rules play no role in the sense that they need not be used by the players of these language-games in making their moves. In such primary language-games as deal with private experiences, the relation of mental events and their "external manifestations" is a logical (necessary) one: one cannot use language to separate the two.[26]

The notion of a physiognomic language-game, according to Hintikka and Hintikka, solves the so-called private language problem, because such languages account for the fact that we can give meaning to and express private sensory phenomenal experiences or mental events in physicalist language. Such a postulation explains passages such as *PI* §244, "How do words *refer* to sensations? . . . Here is one possibility: words are connected with the primitive, the natural expressions of the sensation and used in their place."

Secondary language-games, on the other hand, are those language-games superimposed on primary language-games. They are those rule-governed games in which we use words and expressions rather than develop or give words or expressions their meaning. Thus descriptive secondary language-games (and not all language-games are descriptive) are true or false, verifiable games. Although the connection between primary and secondary language-games is somewhat unclear, Hintikka and Hintikka argue that the distinction is essential for Wittgenstein (a) to explain how we talk about private experiences (through physiognomic language-games) and thus solve the private-language problem, and (b) to account for descriptions of private experiences (in secondary language-games) that are falsifiable.[27]

III

The Hintikkas' interpretation of language-games and their approach to the private language arguments are attractive for a number of reasons. First, this sort of analysis of a language-game, if correct, precludes the ascription to Wittgenstein of any sort of antirealism. Second, it solves the private-language problem without having to admit that the notion of a private experience makes no sense. Third, this notion of the central role of language-games provides an antidote to the Community Views. Language-games are practices. Therefore language-games are not private; but neither are they merely *social* practices. Rather, they are "rule-governed interactions with our non-linguistic environment."[28] Social practices and community agreements are language-games, but there are others. So language-games are constitutive of social practices and community agreements rather than the converse. Fourth, the priority of language-games over rules helps to explain passages in the *PI* such as, "Look on the language-game as the *primary* thing"[29]; or "One can . . . imagine someone's having learnt the game [of chess] without ever learning or formulating the rules"[30]; or "the term 'language-*game*' is meant to bring into prominence the fact that the *speaking* of language is part of an activity, or of a form of life."[31]

However, although the Language-Game Thesis focuses on a crucial Wittgensteinian concept, there are difficulties with the thesis. In this section we shall focus on problems raised by the Hintikkas' primary-secondary language-game distinction. Then in the next section we shall discuss some other questions about this thesis that affect closely the private language arguments.

The primary-secondary language-game distinction, admittedly only implicit in Wittgenstein's writings according to Hintikka and Hintikka, may raise more difficulties than it resolves. First, there are questions about the notion of a primary language-game. While Hintikka and Hintikka claim that language-games are "rule-governed interactions with our nonlinguistic environment," on the other hand they say that "[i]n primary language-games criteria and rules play no role in the sense that they need not be used by the players of these language-games in their moves."[32] But does one want to say that rules play *no* role in physiognomic language-games? Are there no criteria for what "counts" as a natural expression? It cannot be the case that any natural expression can stand for a private experience because as Hintikka and Hintikka quote Wittgenstein, "The rules of grammar are arbitrary in the sense that the rules of a game are arbitrary. We can make them differently. But then it is a different game."[33] How do we then distinguish truly physiognomic language-games from secondary ones?

The problem is not that we cannot, in principle, distinguish between primary and secondary language-games, although their relationship is somewhat unclear; it is rather the postulating of primary language-games. Although they are helpful in explaining some obscure passages in the *PI*, and allegedly solve the private-language problem, they are troublesome in the very way that they solve the private-language dilemma. The notion of a physiognomic language-game and the attending primary-secondary language-game distinction solves the private language problem if one assumes that private experiences are phenomenal objects or sense data. Then, if one denies the possibility of private ostensive definition as a starting point for language, one needs physiognomic language-games to explain how it is that we talk about sense data in everyday language. But the postulating of sense data raises the very kind of problem I read Wittgenstein as trying to avoid in the *PI*. Even if one cannot talk about sense data except in everyday physicalist language, the fact that private experiences are sense data keeps open the wedge to phenomenalism that I read Wittgenstein as being at pains to avoid. I do not think that Wittgenstein is clear about private experiences in his later writings. While he does not deny their existence, he tries to be noncommittal about them and, at best, he vacillates as to their status and nature. But to commit the later Wittgenstein to a sense data theory of any sort seems not to be in keeping with his intentions, since he is so critical of this sort of approach to philosophy, although admittedly it may offer a possible explanation of some, but not all, the passages in the later writings. In Chapter 8 I shall try to make sense out of the notion of a private experience in light of the private language arguments, but what I have to say may or may not be attributable to Wittgenstein either.

The problem with explaining rule-following in primary language-games raises another difficulty: the unclear distinction between the notion of a rule and rule-following, and their relationships to language-games. The notion of a language-game, while helping to clarify what it means to follow a rule, does not account adequately for the distinction between rules and rule-following, and this inadequacy, in turn, becomes particularly problematic in trying to explain the role of rule-following in physiognomic language-games. Hintikka and Hintikka write that in his later work Wittgenstein rejected the centrality of the notion of a rule in favor of language-games as the basic semantical links between language and the world. At the same time Hintikka and Hintikka say that language-games are "complexes of rules."[34]

> . . . the uses of language (the language-games) which Wittgenstein has in mind are not primarily intra-linguistic activities. They are uses *in practice*, i.e., they are rule-governed interactions with our non-linguistic environment.[35]

If a language-game is a complex of rules including or intersecting with nonlinguistic practices, then language-games are tied to rules and rule-following. While the role of a rule in primary language-games is not spelled out by Hintikka and Hintikka, it seems that at least physiognomic language-games employ the notion of a rule in the sense that there is a one-to-one connection between the expression (the primary language-game) and the sense experience, if, as Hintikka and Hintikka claim, primary language-games, as "projective relations," in some way mirror the world.[36] A secondary language-game regulates rule-following practices within a particular game, and within a particular language-game one can distinguish between rules, e.g., the rules of chess, and rule-following activities, e.g., playing chess. But in both primary and secondary language-games, if the distinction can be made between the two, rule-following and nonlinguistic practices function as expressions, games, or practices because of the notion of a rule. Underlying all these activities are rules that are imbedded in expressions, practices, or games (e.g., the rules of chess) and others that are distinct (e.g., "going on in the same way," or "making a mistake"). While it is true that "one can . . . imagine someone's having learnt the game without ever learning or formulating the rules," one cannot dismiss the crucial element of a rule as the basis for the game even when one follows the game rules "blindly" or expresses a sense experience.

Wittgenstein himself talks about distinguishing rules from rule-following. About the priority of the former, one will recall that in §201 he says,

> . . . there is a way of grasping a rule which is *not* an *interpretation*, but which is exhibited in what we call "obeying the rule" and "going against it" in actual cases.
>
> Hence there is an inclination to say: every action according to the rule is an interpretation. But we ought to restrict the term "interpretation" to the substitution of one expression of the rule for another.

About rules, as distinct from interpretations, Wittgenstein says, "[T]he use of the word 'rule' and the use of the word 'same' are interwoven."[37] The notion of a rule entails "same," and thus "difference," so these notions are involved in any rule-governed activity whatsoever.

Moreover, we evaluate languages and language-games. Our evaluative perspective of language-games and even, sometimes, our perspective on the form of life they embody, or the presuppositions that are accepted or have to be accepted as "given" in order for the game to function, suggests that "there is a way of grasping a rule which is not an interpretation." That is, the notion of a rule is distinct from language-games (interpretations) in which rule-following practices are embodied.

A language-game, then, is not merely a "physiognomic framework of spontaneous expressions of sensations"[38] or a nexus of rule-following practices. Underlying the framework of expressions is a one-to-one correlation—a complex mirroring—that presupposes a correct or an incorrect way to mirror. Underlying practices are rules that govern the practices so that one can distinguish between going on correctly and making mistakes. An emphasis on language-games as rule-following practices or rule-governed activities by the Language-Game Thesis does not always so carefully distinguish between rules and rule-following activities. If language-games are "uses in practice," they are by and large rule-following activities or interpretations. Yet, as we shall argue in detail in the next chapter, the notion of a rule is present in all language-games and language-game practices. Rules constitute the conditions for "going on in the same way" and "making a mistake." Rules are not merely embedded within a particular rule-following practice. The notion of a rule is a condition for any language-game because one could not even conceive of a game or a practice without this idea. The Language-Game Thesis does not make that clear.

There is a third problem related to the notion of a primary language-game, the private language arguments, and the notion of a rule. Proponents of the Language-Game Thesis argue that the notion of a private language makes no sense, because following a rule is significant only within the context of a language-game or a wider horizon of human activities. "Even though ostensions and rules can perhaps be private, language-games cannot be."[39] Since Wittgenstein argued that a private language is impossible, he must have held that language-games are conceptually prior. "For if language-games were not prior conceptually to their rules, one could perfectly well define private languages by specifying their private rules."[40] Because (from §202) language-games are practices that encompass a set of linguistic and nonlinguistic behavior, the role a word plays in a language is prescribed by its use in a (nonprivate) language-game. So the uses of words and thus the language cannot be private.

I agree that if language-games are conceptually prior, this would preclude the possibility of a private language. But I question the claim that a *rule* could be private. One of the reasons Hintikka and Hintikka reach that conclusion is that during his middle period Wittgenstein linked rules with ostensive definitions: "Wittgenstein thought that a successful ostensive definition could give to the recipient the *rule* for the use of the word to be defined, or at least an important part of such a rule."[41] According to this logic, if ostensive definitions can be private, then so too can rules. But, as we argued in Chapter 3, the later Wittgenstein rejected the notion of ostension as a starting point for language and argued that making ostensive definitions depends on rules. One cannot make an ostensive definition without engaging in rule-following activities. So unless one can show independently that a rule can be private, Wittgenstein's rejection of ostensive definition does not, in itself, mean that he held that there could be private rules. The point here is that if one substitutes language-games for rules as the basis for language in order to show that a private language is impossible, one needs first to argue that the nature of rules is such that a private rule makes sense.

The most serious difficulty with the postulation of incorrigible physiognomic language-games has to do with their status as incorrigible expressions, their logical link to private phenomenal experiences, and the status of those experiences. If physiognomic language-games are nonverifiable natural expressions or manifestations logically connected with our private experiences and at the same time are understood in such a way that they are not questionable, are these language-games links to reality or merely links to the common ways in which we human beings experience the world? Hintikka and Hintikka contend that the reason that "if a lion could talk, we could not understand him"[42] is because "the sense data which constitute the world of a lion are different from the sense-data of human beings."[43] But then are sense-data part of the natural condition of humankind, part of our common history, or, in Kripke's terms, part of the "brute fact that we generally agree"?

According to the theory of primary language-games, physiognomic language-games are assertions, incorrigible assertions, not merely because they are natural expressions, but also because we share a natural consensus as to what those expressions represent or mean. Otherwise such expressions would not be incorrigible or serve as linguistic manifestations of sense data phenomena in physicalist terms. According to this theory, these physiognomic language-games must manifest what is common in human experience because one questions these expressions only when a particular expression does not agree with what is expected. Herein lies the perplexity. If these primary language-games are the basis of language and secondary language-games, this not only opens up the possibility of linguistic relativism (about which I shall expound in the next section), physiognomic language-games also bring into question Hintikka and Hintikka's repeated claim that language-games are semantic links between language and reality. For if physiognomic language-games are merely assertions of shared common sense-data experiences, they do not refer, and they are not verifiable or confirmable. The link, then, is not between these sorts of language-games and reality, but rather between language-games and common experience or shared responses. Therefore, secondary language-games, that is, language, derived from primary language-games, are based on assertions, not on truth conditions. How, then, can secondary language-games serve as semantical links to reality? How can descriptive language-games, for example, "language-games of verification," be true or false? If physiognomic language-games make incorrigible assertions rather than establish truth conditions and at the same time are *primary* language-games, descriptive secondary language-games can hardly serve as truth conditions for reality. This conclusion is similar to Kripke's, albeit approached in an entirely different manner. I do not think this is the conclusion Hintikka and Hintikka want to reach since it brings into question their central thesis, but it seems to follow from what they say about primary physiognomic language-games.

Had Hintikka and Hintikka shown how Wittgenstein replaces the idea of ostension with the notion of a rule they might not have come to the conclusion that rules can be private. Moreover, that Wittgenstein rejects outright the primacy of ostension, I think, helps to point to the viable possibility that he also rejects the idea of sense data. If this is the case, then the primary-secondary language-game distinction need not be made, and one can talk about all language-games in the way in which Hintikka and Hintikka describe secondary language-games. This is more in keeping with the text of the *PI* at least with those passages we cited in the first section of this chapter, and it avoids the possible implications of physiognomic language-games for the Hintikkas' defense of Wittgenstein as a physicalist. One still must account for public talk about allegedly private experiences, but if "mental" experiences are not merely sense data, this task is not impossible.

Hintikka and Hintikka adopt the language-game thesis for a number of other reasons. One of their most salient points is that language consists of a nexus of linguistic and nonlinguistic rule-governed activities. Words and expressions gain meaning from their uses in a context of such activities. Thus the notion of a rule, like that of ostensive definition, is not rich enough to convey the complexity of language, meaning, and its relation to reality. I think Hintikka and Hintikka are correct in this depiction. I shall argue in Chapter 7, however, that language-games, while essential to the richness of linguistic practices, depend on the notion of a rule.

IV

There are other related perplexities with the Language-Game Thesis, the analysis of which are important for the theses of this book. First, the explanation by Hintikka and Hintikka that language-games play the central role in language and in nonlinguistic human activities leads to a form of "linguistic relativism." Second, this view, like a Community View, creates a private language problem at least on the macro level. These difficulties are connected with a third, that language-games are "forms of life." These problems, taken together, bring into question the Hintikkas' conclusion that "language-games are conceptually prior to their rules."

Defenders of the Language-Game Thesis admit that their interpretation of "[l]ook on the language-game as the *primary* thing" coupled with "Wittgenstein's . . . belief in language as the universal medium"[44] lead to a form of linguistic relativism. From Wittgenstein's claim that "[i]f a lion could talk, we could not understand him" it is argued that Wittgenstein is a sort of relativist about language. According to this view, it is not impossible to imagine other beings (lions), alien beings, or simply other human beings whose language-games and conceptual schemes or "ways of life" are so radically different from our own that we could not understand what they said or if or how they communicated. Their language-games would be such that one could not comprehend what they were talking about or, indeed, realize that the sounds they uttered were forms of speech. Different formations of physiognomic language-games, then, can create "incommensurable conceptual frameworks"[45] that in principle are not and cannot be translatable or understandable to each other. Wittgenstein's notion of a "form of life" as "what has to be accepted, the given"[46] allegedly further supports this conclusion. Language-games are forms of life because the most sophisticated language-games encompass ways of dealing with human activities and the world that entail certain "accepted" presuppositions that themselves cannot be questioned. Thus, another community could adopt certain presuppositions in the language-games they engage in, presuppositions themselves too basic to be questioned, that are incomprehensible to us.

Linguistic relativism leads to a private language problem at least on the "macro" level. This is similar to the problem raised by a Community View but from a different perspective, since according to Hintikka and Hintikka the notion of a language-game does not necessarily derive from community consensus or agreement. In fact, the most important (and controversial) claim of the Language-Game Thesis is that language-games, unlike community consensus, establish truth conditions rather than serve as assertability conditions. Whether or not this is the case, and we have discussed the difficulties with this position, if language-games are forms of life such that the language-game of an alien community could be incomprehensible, then the Language-Game Thesis, like a Community View, allows the possibility of private languages on the macro level.

Was Wittgenstein a linguistic relativist? Despite the Hintikkas' persuasive arguments, Wittgenstein's alleged linguistic relativism is much in debate. The text, §206 in the *Investigations*, "The common behaviour of mankind is the system of reference by means of which we interpret an unknown language,"[47] is often cited in support of the view that Wittgenstein was not. Hintikka and Hintikka, however, translate §206 as: "People's shared way of acting [or, more literally: 'The shared human way of acting'] is the frame of reference by means of which we interpret an unknown language."[48] If a group of aliens had a shared way of acting that was radically different from ours, the frame of reference (the activities and practices of that community) could not guide an interpretation of their language-games and thus their language.

In contrast to Hintikka and Hintikka I want to point out that it is surely the case that Wittgenstein argued vehemently against the notion of a private language. So even Wittgenstein appears to be a linguistic relativist, if relativism creates a private language problem, it is not out of keeping with the spirit of the later Wittgenstein to question this thesis even if it means admitting that Wittgenstein might have been inconsistent on this point. Moreover, there is another way to read the "lion" text that does not lend support to his alleged linguistic relativism. In saying, "If a lion could talk we could not understand him" Wittgenstein could be implying that the reason we cannot understand a lion is that the lion's behavior and way of life are so different that merely hearing his words gives us little in the way of clues to the references and meanings of his expressions. Should we get to know the lion's habits, his socialization process, and the way he deals with the world, we could understand him. So Wittgenstein could be arguing that while languages are not incommensurable in principle with each other, one's "natural history" plays a crucial role in the way we use words. Alien cultures are comprehensible, but without knowledge of the natural history of another culture (or the society of lions), one cannot, in fact, always understand an alien language.[49]

Linguistic relativism is related to another philosophical position, linguistic idealism. The linguistic relativist argues that different communities or different beings can have incommensurable language-games. From Wittgenstein's statement that *"[e]ssence* is expressed by grammar"[50] a relativist may conclude that there can be radically different grammars and therefore radically different "expressions of essence." The very "bedrock" expressions of each language can be so different that no language is translatable. The linguistic idealist argues that "essence is *created* by grammar."[51] This view contends, in brief, that "[t]he human possession of concepts . . . the existence of concepts . . . depend[s] on human linguistic practice."[52] Recalling the discussions in Chapters 4 and 5, both Kripke's and Wright's interpretations of Wittgenstein commit Wittgenstein to a form of linguistic idealism because, according to these views, one can never get at the world or truths about the world. What one takes to be reality or truths about reality are matters of linguistic conventions based on community consensus.

Hintikka and Hintikka argue that Wittgenstein is not a linguistic idealist. Why, then, do they claim he is a relativist? Suppose as a traveler I come upon a group of alien beings. These beings write things down, albeit in a strange code, and appear to communicate to each other. According to linguistic relativism these aliens could "express essence" in ways incommensurable to mine. But even if the framework of a shared way of acting out of which the aliens constitute their language or whatever they use to communicate (if, in fact, their noises are meant to be means of communication) is radically different from mine, if the aliens and I share another common frame of reference, i.e., a common reality, this opens a wedge for my getting at what the aliens mean by their expressions even though their *way* of "expressing essence" is distinct from mine.[53]

Linguistic relativism should be a questionable position from the point of view of the Language-Game Thesis since one of the major aims of that thesis is to question linguistic idealism by arguing that language-games constitute the semantical links between language and the world. If language-games *do* constitute these links, then even allegedly incommensurable language-games would have some common subject matter for their language. Linguistic relativism, then, is inconsistent with the Hintikkas' interpretation of Wittgenstein as a physicalist, because according to the presuppositions of most physicalists it is not inconceivable that one could grasp an "alien" language-game.

V

The discussion of language-games relates to another notoriously difficult Wittgensteinian term, "form of life." This term has been defined as follows: "Because they are patterns, regularities, configurations, Wittgenstein calls them forms; and because they are patterns in the fabric of human existence and activity on earth, he calls them forms of life."[54] Even given that definition, Wittgenstein uses the expression in a number of ways. Sometimes he speaks as if forms of life are specific activities or particular kinds of activities, behaviors, tendencies, or ways of dealing with experience. For instance, "Can only those hope who can talk? Only those who have mastered the use of language. That is to say the phenomena of hope are modes of this complicated form of life."[55] Or, "Why should it always be pretending that is taking place—this very special pattern which recurs in the weave of our lives?"[56] Usually, however, Wittgenstein reserves the term "form of life" to talk about more general but basic human activities or ways of life such as social or cultural practices, religion, or even language. For example, he says, "Why shouldn't one form of life culminate in an utterance of belief in a Last Judgement?"[57] Other philosophers claim that "a form of life is a pattern of meaningful behavior in so far as this is constituted by a group."[58] This supports the conclusion that the collection of activities of a community, e.g., its social practices, is a candidate for a form of life.

From "[a]nd to imagine a language means to imagine a form of life,"[59] it is said that language itself may be a form of life. From "[h]ere the term 'language-game' is meant to bring into prominence the fact that the *speaking* of language is part of an activity, or of a form of life" Hintikka and Hintikka argue that language-games are forms of life.

On another level Wittgenstein sometimes talks as if a form of life is the "bedrock," the very precondition for there being language, language-games, communities, religion, or any sort of meaningful human activity at all. For example, Wittgenstein says, "Now I would like to regard this certainty, not as something akin to hastiness or superficiality, but as a form of life . . . something . . . beyond being justified or unjustified; as it were, as something animal."[60] Accordingly, one could give a more "organic" account of forms of life as the bedrock of our biological nature from which human activities develop, "something typical of a living being . . . organic."[61] Or forms of life could be primitive concepts constituting a "common history" that underlies human activities, and more specifically, language.[62] Forms of life, then, can be particular ways of dealing with experience, more general presuppositions underlying a practice or a kind of approach to human activity, or the very conditions for human activity.

The problem with the notion "form of life" is that one sometimes talks about *the* form of life and other times about forms of life. Forms of life, then, are often confused with the "bedrock," the very basis for there being human activities at all. Those who defend a Community View sometimes make this confusion by arguing that community consensus is *a* form of life (and since there can be any number of disparate communities, there can be any number of forms of life), and then argue further that such agreements are *the* bedrock, that is, the basis for there being a community or human social interaction at all. Similarly, the Language-Game Thesis appears to claim both that a language-game or a set of language-games is a form of life, and that there could be any number of these; yet at the same time the thesis claims that the notion of a language-game is the bedrock because one cannot go beyond them.

Whether or not Wittgenstein would agree, a distinction between forms of life and "bedrock," the very conditions for their being forms of life, is a desirable one and necessary both to avoid linguistic relativism and a private language problem as well as to clarify the distinction between the notion of a rule and rule-following practices. Forms of life delineate rule-following activities or interpretations, e.g., language-games and practices, all of which depend on the acceptance of certain presuppositions or agreements that serve as the framework or justification for the language-game or practice. But, as I shall argue in the next chapter, the notion of a rule is the ground for whatever one wants to call "forms of life." It is a "bedrock" beyond which one cannot question because that notion is itself a condition for the activities of questioning and evaluating to take place. Most importantly, as we shall see, the notion of a rule rather than that of a language-game more adequately accounts for the conditions for rule-governed activities. It solves the private language problem on the macro level, avoids linguistic relativism, and allows one to make a viable interpretation out of the notion of forms of life without contradiction or inconsistency. Thus it is adequate to explain the "bedrock" of activities of all sorts. This conclusion is not out of keeping with the *Philosophical Investigations*, in particular, because, "'How am I able to obey a rule?' . . . If I have exhausted the justifications I have reached bedrock, and my spade is turned. Then I am inclined to say: "This is simply what I do.'"[63]

VI

The notion of a language-game explains the ways in which human activities are interwoven so that language is not an isolated human phenomenon but operates within the context of other human activities that give words their meanings and accounts for creativity in language. Whether or not the notion of a language-game adequately accounts for a link between language and reality is debatable, but this conclusion is no more questionable than an antirealist interpretation of Wittgenstein. Contrary to a Community View, it explains more adequately Wittgenstein's emphasis on the variety of uses of words and expressions—a variety that should include the use of sentences as facts as well as assertions. It is probably more likely that Wittgenstein was neither a realist nor an antirealist, but to argue that would require another book. Important as the Language-Game Thesis is, however, it has not demonstrated that a rule, but not a language-game, could be private, it has not satisfactorily responded to the problem of linguistic relativism, or solved all the ramifications of the private language problem on the macro level. The examination of the Language-Game Thesis, however, has highlighted the problem of linguistic relativism. The discussion has clarified various formulations of Wittgenstein's expression, "form of life." Employed with caution this expression is useful in distinguishing a variety of human activities, underlying all of which is a bedrock without which human life and interaction would not be possible. In the next chapter I shall argue that the notion of a rule is this bedrock, and that such a notion clears up some of the confusion concerning "form of life" and solves the puzzle of linguistic relativism.

Notes

1. Merrill Hintikka and Jaakko Hintikka, *Investigating Wittgenstein*, p. 212, italics removed.
2. Ibid., p. 196.
3. Wittgenstein, *PI*, §7.
4. Hintikka and Hintikka, *Investigating Wittgenstein*, p. 189.
5. Wittgenstein, *PI*, §179.
6. Ibid., §43.
7. Ibid., §23.
8. Ibid.
9. Ibid., Part II, p. 226.

10. This leads Henry Finch to declare that "[l]anguage-games are the fundamental 'units of sense' in the *Investigations* . . . They are the absolute starting point." Henry L. Finch, *Wittgenstein: The Later Philosophy* (Atlantic Highlands, NJ: Humanities Press, 1977), pp. 69, 74.
11. Wittgenstein, *PI*, §7.
12. Hintikka and Hintikka, p. 220.
13. Ibid., p. 190.
14. Ibid., p. 196.
15. Ibid., p. 199.
16. Ibid., p. 201.
17. See Dallas M. High, *Language, Persons, and Belief* (New York: Oxford University Press, 1967), p. 102, and Finch, *Wittgenstein*, Chapter 6.
18. Hintikka and Hintikka, p. 176.
19. Ibid., p. 190.
20. Wittgenstein, *PI*, §10.
21. Hintikka and Hintikka, *Investigating Wittgenstein*, p. 226.
22. Ibid., p. 247.
23. Ibid., p. 251.
24. Ibid., p. 219. See also Wittgenstein, *PI*, §23.
25. Wittgenstein, "Notes for Lectures on 'Private Experiences' and 'Sense Data,'" ed. Rush Rhees, *Philosophical Review* 77 (1968): 297, quoted in Hintikka and Hintikka as proof of what should constitute a primary language-game, p. 279.
26. Hintikka and Hintikka, *Investigating Wittgenstein*, p. 274.
27. Ibid., pp. 256–267, and Chapter 11 for a discussion of physiognomic language-games, and the primary-secondary language-game distinction.
28. Hintikka and Hintikka, *Investigating Wittgenstein*, p. 195.
29. Wittgenstein, *PI*, §656.
30. Ibid., §31.
31. Ibid., §23.
32. Hintikka and Hintikka, *Investigating Wittgenstein*, p. 274.
33. Wittgenstein, *Wittgenstein's Lectures, Cambridge 1930–1932*, ed. Desmond Lee (Oxford: Basil Blackwell, 1980), p. 57, reprinted in Hintikka and Hintikka, *Investigating Wittgenstein*, p. 236.
34. Hintikka and Hintikka, *Investigating Wittgenstein*, p. 198.
35. Ibid., p. 195.
36. Ibid., p. 234.
37. Wittgenstein, *PI*, §225.
38. Hintikka and Hintikka, *Investigating Wittgenstein*, p. 275.
39. Ibid., p. 242.
40. Ibid., p. 243.
41. Ibid., p. 180.
42. Wittgenstein, *PI*, Part II, p. 223.
43. Hintikka and Hintikka, *Investigating Wittgenstein*, p. 252.
44. Ibid., p. 21.
45. See Dancy, "Alien Concepts," pp. 283–300, for an interesting analysis of this problem. In this article Dancy is talking about linguistic idealism, but his discussion of idealism is similar to the Hintikkas' definition of linguistic relativism. See the discussion to follow.

46. Wittgenstein, *PI*, Part II, p. 226.
47. See Anscombe, "The Question of Linguistic Idealism," pp. 188–215. Anscombe is arguing that Wittgenstein is not a linguistic idealist. But, as I shall argue, if Wittgenstein is not a linguistic idealist, it is difficult to maintain he is a relativist. Anscombe appeals to *PI*, Part II, p. 230, to support her case.

If anyone believes that certain concepts are absolutely the right ones, and that having different concepts would mean not realizing something that we realize—then let him imagine certain very general facts of nature to be different from what we are used to, and the formation of concepts different from usual ones will become intelligible to him.

48. Hintikka and Hintikka, *Investigating Wittgenstein*, p. 188.
49. See John Churchill, "'If a lion could talk,'" *Philosophical Investigations* 12 (1989): 308–324 for the articulation and defense of this point.
50. Wittgenstein, *PI*, §371.
51. Anscombe, p. 188.
52. Ibid., p. 190, my emphasis.
53. See Dancy, "Alien Concepts," pp. 283–300.
54. Hanna Pitkin, *Wittgenstein and Justice* (Berkeley, CA: University of California Press, 1972), p. 132, quoted in Nicholas F. Gier, "Wittgenstein and Forms of Life," *Philosophy of the Social Sciences* 10 (1980): 244.
55. Wittgenstein, *PI*, p. 174.
56. Ibid., p. 229.
57. Wittgenstein, *Lectures and Conversations on Aesthetics, Psychology, and Religious Belief*, ed. C. Barrett (Berkeley, CA: University of California Press, 1966), p. 58.
58. Finch, *Wittgenstein*, pp. 90–91.
59. Wittgenstein, *PI*, §19. See Gier, "Wittgenstein and Forms of Life," for further clarification of the notion of a form of life in Wittgenstein's writings.
60. Wittgenstein, *On Certainty*, trans. G. E. M. Anscombe (New York: Macmillan and Co., 1958), p. 358–359.
61. John Hunter, "Forms of Life in Wittgenstein's *Philosophical Investigations*," *American Philosophical Quarterly* 5 (1968): 233–243.
62. See High, *Language, Persons, and Belief*, p. 102. Nicholas Gier also may hold this view. On this point Gier says,

Here [in §23] it is not clear whether the speaking of language is a form of life or only part of a more basic activity which is a form of life. The following passage . . . indicate[s] that the correct interpretation must be the latter.

Giving grounds, however, justifying the evidence, comes to an end;—but the end is not certain propositions striking use immediately as true, i.e., it is not a kind of *seeing* on our part; it is our acting, which lies at the bottom (*Grunde*) of the language-game. [*On Certainty*, 204]

Gier, "Wittgenstein and Forms of Life," p. 246.
63. Wittgenstein, *PI*, §217.

7

"The Language . . . Which Only I Myself Can Understand"

Community Views and the Language-Game Thesis are not without intractable ambiguities. It is a difficult task, however, to present an alternative to either view that is consistent with Wittgenstein's later writings and is itself philosophically viable. Such an alternative must accomplish the following:

1. Construct an alternative to the thesis that "the general practice of the community is constitutive of its linguistic rules," an alternative that is consistent with the *Philosophical Investigations*.
2. Develop an adequate private language argument that avoids linguistic relativism.
3. Offer a plausible explanation of Wittgenstein's alleged conventional antirealism, or, justify the basis for saying that Wittgenstein does not hold such a view.
4. Explain why language is not based merely on assertability conditions.
5. Show why it is that primitive reactions, community consensus, and/or social practices are not the "bedrock."

This chapter will present an alternative to a Community View and the Language-Game Thesis. In exploring the relation of a language rule to the possibility of a private language it shall be argued that the notion of a rule and its role in a language preclude the possibility of a necessarily private language. We shall call these private language arguments the Rule Arguments. Such arguments solve the private language problem without reifying intentions or committing Wittgenstein explicitly to realism or antirealism. They bring into question linguistic idealism and circumvent linguistic relativism. In contrast both to a Community View and the Language-Game Thesis, I shall argue that "linguistic rules are constitutive of the general practice of the community" and the basis for language-games as well. It will be concluded that "the brute fact that we generally agree," social practices, and language-games depend on the notion of a rule, which is the "bedrock" of language and human activities.

I

Let us try to imagine an extreme situation where, *per hypothesis*, in developing a language, a person, S, has no access to rules or guidelines for uttering sounds, and where S is unable to develop any such conventions. In this instance S would merely utter sounds at random, some of which would occur in the presence of sensations S was experiencing. This is not the same as making private primitive ostensive definitions. For in that case S would operate under at least one associative directive, namely, "Utter a sound when a sensation occurs," and this sound denotes the object at hand at the time of the utterance. In this instance, however, S is to operate under no rules at all. Uttering sounds would be a chance act not necessarily related to the occurrence of a sensation that might be experienced at the time of the utterance. Obviously, then, without applying any patterns to his utterances so that S consistently uses sounds in some way, a language cannot develop in any sense.

This illustration may be developed into an argument showing that under the conditions specified, a private language is an absurdity. But this argument is in one sense trivial because in order to carry it out one must stipulate conditions which are themselves almost absurd. One must imagine that S would *try* to develop a language when he does not even understand that making sounds is a significant act. There is an obvious distinction, then, between uttering sounds with some regularity and using sounds as words. However, it will turn out that distinction does not depend on differentiating between developing a language in isolation and learning a language in a community.

The foregoing also illustrates the importance of rules even in simple language-forming situations. In making ostensive definitions, one first learns that making sounds is in itself a meaningful act, and one understands, in some simple sense, the idea behind some referring principle in order even to denote a particular with a sound. Making ordinary ostensive definitions requires that one can consistently reassociate the same sound with the same kind of object. The grounds for making ostensive definitions, then, are not merely sound-object associations. Rather, reviewing the arguments of Chapter 3, to make ostensive definitions one must first learn or have at hand certain "principles" of association which prescribe formulas for linking particular sound-object associations into definitions of classes of phenomena. For if one does not grasp some idea of reiterated pointing, for example, one cannot even *seem* consistently to reapply the ostensive associations to similar objects. David Hume noticed this, and his "qualities" of the imagination are simple associative principles which enable one to compare impressions and ideas, to reapply sounds to similar impressions, and thus to name ideas. Moreover, the context of the association, e.g., the language-game including the kind of object or phenomenon to be named, is also important for ostensive definition to make consistent sense.

To use sounds to express words, e.g., class terms, which are consistently reapplicable to a variety of similar objects, one must first understand "how to go on" and "how to go on in the same way." In speaking one uses certain principles or patterns that can be reapplied in new speaking contexts. Consistently using a word or expression according to certain patterns entails that one understands or can understand what would count as an incorrect use of a word and what would count as using the word in the same way on different occasions. What we shall call rules of a language are these patterns for the correct application of words and expressions in that language. They are guidelines for "what counts as going on in the same way." A language rule, then, may be defined as a convention governing the uses of words or expressions in a language so that not every utterance of a sound as a word or expression constitutes a correct (or incorrect) use of that word or expression.

In talking about following a rule Wittgenstein says that "[i]t is not possible that there should have been only one occasion on which someone obeyed a rule."[1] Wittgenstein does not necessarily mean that literally there could not be a case where a specific rule was obeyed only once. Rather, the passage can be interpreted as saying that a rule specifies the formal conditions under which one may repeatedly use words and sentences consistently and in the same way. For sounds to be used as words these sounds must be used according to certain patterns which can be correctly or incorrectly applied in a multitude of ways on a variety of different occasions.[2] A rule, then, specifies the parameters of reiterative rule-following activities. So a rule could *in fact* be obeyed only once; but a rule specifies conditions for rule-following which allow the rule in question to be followed an infinite number of times.[3]

What sorts of "rules" would result if the criteria for the use of a word followed no patterns? Without that characteristic, any use of a word would be said to "follow some rule" and thus no use would be either appropriate or inappropriate. Hence it could not be said that they were rules at all, and the resulting "language" would be like S's, since it makes no sense to speak of the "randomness" or the "logical indeterminacy" of a rule. Therefore if "speaking a language" is not to be defined as "uttering random noises," the notion of a rule is necessary to the formation or learning of any language.

II

If it is true that some sorts of rules at least in the form of patterns for the repeatable application of sounds are necessary for the construction, development, and/or learning of a language, the question to be answered is: Is a "private rule" and hence a private rule-guided language possible? Can one construct, develop, or learn a language that follows rules understood only by the language user even when the language is heard or read by persons other than its speaker? The issue is twofold. First, can one derive a language from one's own *rules*, in the absence of standards other than one's own ideas for using linguistic patterns? A Community View and the Language-Game Thesis argue that one cannot. Second, if, counter to a Community View, a language could be so derived, is such a language a private language? Hintikka and Hintikka suggest that rules *could* be private and thus that if rules are the basis for language, there could be a private rule-guided language.[4]

Recalling Chapter 4, we argue that it might be possible for a person, Robinson Crusoe, to think he is following a rule without ever knowing or confirming by some independent standard of verification whether he is actually doing so. Accordingly, so long as he could set aside some of his think-rule-following activities as criteria with which to judge further uses of words, Robinson could make comparisons between those "objective" rule applications and his present word usage, correcting himself with what he thought were proper applications of his criteria. What was at issue (in the question of whether Robinson could develop a language in isolation) was whether or not Robinson, by himself, could distinguish the notion of a *rule* from his rule-following activities, a notion to evaluate both his rule-following standards and his rule-following activities. Could Robinson develop his own rules, and if so, would the rules and the language derived therein be private, that is, logically private so that it would be impossible for persons other than him to understand the language due to the nature of its construction by the speaker?

First we shall discuss the question, "Can the notion of a rule be developed and function without appealing to external standards?" If so, then this is a counter-argument to a Community View. Then in the next section we shall apply this discussion to the question, "Can there be a private language in any sense?" Let us examine some situations where one tries to develop a language privately from one's own conventions. Let us discuss the case where Janet Crusoe, Robinson's cousin, tries to develop a language about her sensations by herself from scratch. In this instance whenever Janet feels what she thinks is a certain kind of sensation, she tries to distinguish it from other kinds of sensations. To make these distinctions Janet must understand that, in general, using sounds to refer to sensations is a meaningful activity, and in so differentiating the first kind of sensation from other kinds of sensations Janet must think she is employing certain patterns for associating like sensations. Let us suppose that Janet calls the first kind of sensation she experiences E, and let us call the first pattern of association Janet thinks of as "following rule x."

It would appear that if Janet thinks she is following some rule x for reidentifying like objects, she must have some idea of the supposed contravention of x, x'. In this instance Janet must have some idea of what it would be to name what seemed to be similar sensations with different names or to call unlike sensations by the same name, to mix up names, or even not to refer to her sensations at all. Even if Janet only *seems* to be following a rule x, she must have some idea of what it would be to think she was not following this rule in order for the former to make sense to her. Otherwise she would have no basis for trying correctly to rename sensations, for there would be no reason why Janet could not call any sensation E. Without the idea of "seems different from" she would have no reason systematically to differentiate one sensation from another. Therefore Janet must have or develop some counter-principle to "following think-rule x," e.g., "follow think-rule x'," or even another rule-following activity, x_1, "do not follow think-rule x," by which she can judge whether she thinks she is following rule x.

This is true even in simple identification and naming situations. Let us suppose that Janet experiences only two kinds of sensations, let us call them e and e', and no others. In one instance Janet experiences these two kinds of sensations simultaneously. On this occasion she notices that e and e' seem different and calls the first "E" and the second "E'." However, Janet's ability to reidentify these sensations and successfully and consistently reapply the sounds "E" and "E'" as words depends on her having some understanding of what it is to identify or refer to a sensation with a sound and on her having some idea of what counts as a correct, and as an incorrect, application of these sounds to these sensations, what might count as the same on a different sensation. Even if Janet only thinks she is naming her sensations correctly, she must use the ideas of "seems the same" and "seems different." Otherwise "E" and "E'" will apply indifferently to sensations e and e', and neither Janet nor anyone else will be able to identify e and e' by these sounds.

To make this situation more difficult let us suppose that Janet experiences only one kind of sensation, e, and never experiences another kind of sensation. And let us suppose that she has no idea of the possible existence of sensations other than e, such as f, and that Janet experiences sensation e continuously so that she cannot experientially compare "having a sensation" to "not having a sensation." Janet utters the sound "E." Obviously Janet could repeatedly utter "E" whenever she liked and one could not say whether or not she was referring to her sensation or that she was wrong in the way in which she named her sensations, because all of Janet's sensations are alike and continuous. But in this instance Janet has, at best, merely a "language" consisting of one sound, "E." She has no idea of how to use "E" to refer to her sensation, nor has she any idea of what it would be to misname it.

If Janet is truly to name her e sensation, she must have some idea of how to refer to a sensation with a sound and she must have some idea of how to misname the sensation, e.g., to call e "F." If "E" is to be a word in a language in which there are other words and if "E" is to apply to a certain kind of sensation, e, rather than merely to Janet's sensation, then Janet must be able to determine whether she is naming what *seems* to be a continuous identical sensation correctly. She must be able to understand what it is to misapply other words to her sensation and to use the word "E" to refer to sensations other than her own. In other words, Janet must have or develop at least two think-rules such as Rule X, "apply the same sound to what seem to be similar sensations," and Rule Y, "apply different sounds to similar sensations," two think-rules with which she can decide whether she seems to be correctly or incorrectly applying the sound "E" and other sounds as words to her sensation. Therefore, even in the most simple language situation Janet must use at least two "think-rules," "seems the same" or "seems correct" and "seems different," in order successfully to reidentify and distinguish objects or sensations and meaningfully apply sounds as words.

A Community View grants that Janet by herself can distinguish between thinking she is following a rule and thinking she is not doing so. According to at least some versions, what Janet lacks is the distinction between rules and rule-following so that she can evaluate her think-rule-following activities. In contrast, I want to argue that if Janet can distinguish between thinking she is following a rule and not doing so, she is distinguishing between what seems to her to be correct from what seems incorrect in the application of sounds as words. In being able to develop and make those distinctions she implicitly assumes a regularity of the think-rule-following practices she engages in. This consistency is not dependent on Janet's particular rule-following activities or on how she develops her own idiolectic speech habits, but it is the basis for any sort of rule-following activity. So if Janet thinks she is following a rule, she is implicitly applying a rule in these activities. Thus if one grants that Janet can distinguish between seeming to follow a rule and not doing so, a point granted by a Community View, then Janet is at least implicitly appealing to rules that are independent of her particular practices.

Can Janet develop and employ "think-rules" and thereby distinguish what seems correct from what seems incorrect, a distinction that depends on her being able at least implicitly to distinguish the notions of "correct" from "incorrect"? In the foregoing we pointed out that Janet cannot say that one sensation seems like another, and hence that both should be called "E," unless she has some understanding of the distinction between "seems the same" and "seems different" to make comparisons. In deciding whether she is following a rule, Janet cannot even think she is, or is not, following a rule if she does not have some grasp of notions by which she can compare "seems the same sensation" to "seems different," and "I think I am following rule x" to "I think I am making a mistake." Janet could not even *think* she was using rule x to identify her sensations, nor could she reapply a rule unless she was able to separate a seemingly correct from a seemingly erroneous application of a sound so that she knows what counts as "using a word in the same way," or "applying rule x correctly" and can use rule x consistently and repeatedly in the implicit context of rule x'. Otherwise any application of rule x could count as "correct," and Janet would not be following rules or developing a language at all.

Following Wittgenstein's claim that "to *think* one is obeying a rule is not to obey a rule. Hence it is not possible to obey a rule 'privately':

otherwise thinking one was obeying a rule would be the same thing as obeying is,"[5] a number of philosophers argue that whatever it is that Janet is doing, she cannot develop a language merely from her own "think-rules" in isolation from, or out of context with, some sorts of independent standards with which she can distinguish what she *thinks* is a correct application of the sound "E," for example, from what she *thinks* is an incorrect application. This is because without such independent standards Janet has only memories of her past uses of "E," and thus she has no way to evaluate which uses are correct or incorrect ones. According to this point of view, Janet has "no criterion of correctness. One would like to say: whatever is going to seem right to me is right."[6] This is "as if someone were to buy several copies of the morning paper to assure himself that what it said was true."[7] The general idea is that one cannot evaluate rule-following without having at hand rules that are independent of rule-following since in these cases one has no criteria for comparison that are different from x. Any "rule" would be all right and indeed could be called "x."[8]

There are good reasons, however, to think that this argument is inappropriate to this case. Janet *does* have independent criteria that she uses in constructing and evaluating the application of her think-rules, the criteria she uses for distinguishing following a think-rule and seeming to misapply it. For example, in trying to name pain Janet may have some criteria for feeling intensity, other criteria for pain duration, and still other criteria for exactness of the comparison between two sensations. In all cases, however, being able to apply sounds consistently serves Janet in a general way as a rule to establish a variety of criteria to evaluate her own variety of rule applications. Moreover, there is no reason, no good reason, why Janet could not set aside a set of think-rules, e.g., Y, Y_1, Y_2, etc., not merely as rule-applications, that are objective to her particular applications of these rules. Janet has some notion of consistency, so that she can judge whether she is "going on in the same way," and she can "verify" that by comparing her applications of a think-rule to her "independent" set of rules. Of course Janet can "cheat" and change her rules or allow exceptions, but this happens under more public circumstances as well. In the foregoing situation, if someone were to translate Janet's language and suggest corrections to her identifications and uses of words and rules, she could distinguish (1) what seems to her to be right (think-rule applications), (2) her "objective" rules she has set aside to evaluate her applications, and (3) what, by some other public standard, was considered a correct use of rules and words.[9]

How, then, is one to understand §202 ("to *think* one is obeying a rule is not to obey a rule")? In this context it is plausible that Wittgenstein is not contrasting individual think-rules with social practices. Rather, what Wittgenstein may be saying is that "if rule-following were private in the sense of being a condition or process of consciousness, then self-ascriptions of rule-following would be infallible."[10] That is, if rule-following is merely idiosyncratic dispositions or nonreflective "processes," or habits, one would be merely trying to follow think-rules. Language development including the uses of signs as words entails being able not merely to engage in rule-following activities, but also to evaluate one's linguistic habits and dispositions in terms of criteria for the proper and improper uses of words. This process does not preclude a context where one learns language through social training where the rules for correct and incorrect applications of signs as words have been established. But the point is that the notion of a rule is not necessarily identified with a *social* practice. What Wittgenstein may be implying is that Janet, for example, needs independent criteria to distinguish what she thinks is right in a particular case. But the distinction between what Janet thinks is right and what is right does not preclude her making these distinctions herself so long as she can separate criteria for evaluation from particular applications of rules.

A communitarian will respond that while it is true that we make the distinction between the notion of a rule and following a rule (we have just been doing so), conditions for making these distinctions are missing for persons in isolation from social practices. But, as we saw in Chapter 4, a community is in no better position than Janet to arrive at the notion of a rule. If a rule reflects, or is developed out of, habits and dispositions there is no reason that Janet cannot develop this notion by herself from her habits and dispositions. If, as Wittgenstein declares in §201 ("What this shews is that there is a way of grasping a rule which is *not* an *interpretation*"), rules are normative conditions for rule-following and not merely interpretations, consensus is neither a necessary nor a sufficient condition for the development of a rule. So Janet is in no better or worse position than a community to develop a language.

III

To review, the argument to this point has been the following:

(1) In principle, one can develop a language from one's own rules without appealing to standards other than one's own, so long as one can distinguish the notions of "seems correct" from "seems incorrect" and

consistently apply these ideas by setting up one's own independent standards of correctness.

(2) Accordingly, these distinctions are necessary conditions for one's developing language and therefore are not dependent on the particular rules one uses in a specific language.

(3) The possible privacy of a language, then, depends on whether the notion of consistency or the concepts of "same" and "difference" could be private, and it is clear that they cannot. If Janet employs rules in her so-called private rule language, these think-rules are at least implicitly tied up with the notions of "same" and "difference" even when Janet uses what she thinks are merely her own rules. Because these ideas are interrelated with the notion of a rule, they are part of any rule Janet uses or any kind of syntax she develops. They are necessary for using a word or speaking a language. Hence, a language cannot be developed without appealing to, or implicitly employing, concepts that are general ideas present in any language and that are not developed merely within the language in question. Even if Janet develops a completely new syntax so that her language does not employ grammatical patterns familiar to speakers of, say, a Germanic language, her language will be internally coherent and the grammatical patterns or rules her syntax generates would be used repeatedly and consistently, whatever "applying a rule correctly" would mean in this syntax. It is this kind of repeatability and consistency that are necessary for any language. These ideas are independent of any think-rules Janet might have developed in the sense that they are not derived from her own rules or rule-following and do not depend upon the particular way Janet follows a rule in a specific instance.

A language cannot be called a necessarily private language merely if it was spoken by, or in the mind of, only one person, because these circumstances do not necessarily preclude incomprehensibility. A rule cannot be logically private in the sense that it is incomprehensible *per se* to persons other than the speaker of the language. A so-called private-rule language is not a private language, because the construction or development of one's own personal rules or even of a complete personal and unique syntax depends on one's applying sounds consistently and distinguishing what seems correct from what seems different. This is the basis for one's acting in any organized way whatsoever. If the idea of a rule is an integral part of a language, then a language that is incomprehensible to persons other than its speaker because of the way in which it is structured is impossible in principle. Whenever Janet speaks, in using a language rule she speaks or writes with a repeatable consistency that allows the language she has developed to be understood by others.

Let us specify the conclusion that the notion of a rule, and that notion alone, precludes the possibility of a private language by relating it to another example. Let us suppose that Robinson Crusoe (on his desert island) developed a language as we have described it in the last section, that is, a language based on a grammar developed by him alone and whose subject matter was merely his sensations. Moreover, Robinson is a strange person who experiences unique, unusual, and weird sensations. Then let us suppose that Q came to Robinson's island. Robinson might keep his language a secret by never uttering its words aloud or otherwise revealing it. But let us specify that Robinson spoke his language to Q. The point of this argument is that *if* Robinson speaks his language, then by observing P's patterns of word use Q could, at least in principle, interpret this language even though Q could not observe the subject matter of Robinson's language or even experience similar sensations. This is because unless Robinson incorporated certain patterns or rules into his way of speaking he could not develop a language, and these patterns of speaking, because they are *patterns*, give Q a foothold into understanding this language if Q hears or reads it. In order to use language rules Robinson *must* act with a consistency and a regularity, and it is the consistency and regularity that allow Robinson's language to be comprehensible to others. Thus Robinson's language is at least theoretically understandable to others even when he has created the rules employed in that language by himself, even when the subject matter is perceivable only to himself, and even when the language exists only in his own mind.

One might object to this conclusion as follows. Are patterns of speaking enough to give Q a foothold into Robinson's language? For example, suppose Q perceived only the colors blue and black, and suppose Robinson used the color term "yellow." Even if Q understood that yellow was a color term in Robinson's language, would that be enough to give Q a full comprehension of Robinson's nonblack and blue color terms?[11]

The short answer is that even if the color yellow is not experienced by Q, that Q can understand that it is a color term is enough to understand Robinson's uses of nonblack and blue color terms. Most blind people understand what one means by "yellow" and other color terms even while never experiencing that color. More will be said about this kind of objection in the next section.

IV

There are a number of possible objections to the foregoing argument. Margaret Gilbert points out that the private language arguments sometimes conflate two points. First, the arguments show that meanings or concepts are in principle shareable,[12] that is, "[1] If a person P1 uses a word in a certain sense (with certain semantic properties) then there could be another person, P2 who uses that word in that sense (with those properties)."[13] However, Gilbert contends, this conclusion is different from saying, "[2] If one individual, P1, uses a word in a certain sense, then some other individual P2 should in principle be able to discover that P1 is doing so."[14] The former, [1], says that "concepts . . . are objective particulars"[15] such that different persons could share or understand the same concepts even if they had different experiences and even if they never communicated with each other. The latter, [2], which Gilbert calls the "meaning-identifiability" thesis, states that when one uses a word, the meaning of that word can, in principle, be discovered by another. Gilbert argues that while [1] is intuitively obvious, it is by no means clear that the latter claim [2] is true.[16]

The foregoing arguments in this chapter have concluded that

[0] because all languages are rule-governed, and
[1a] because "[t]he use of the word 'rule' and the use of the word 'same' are interwoven,"[17] (a version of claim [1]), therefore:
[2a] any language one creates, develops, or speaks could in principle be understood by another (a version of claim [2]).

[1a] argues that the notions of sameness and difference (a) are the basis for rules and rule-following and (b) are, in Gilbert's terminology, "objective particulars," that is, shareable concepts. Because sameness and difference are objective particulars and are the basis for rule-governed activities, I have concluded

[2b] in principle one can understand the rule-governed activities of another, that is, one can get at the rule or pattern or grammar of another.

So it is possible, logically possible, to understand the language of another and therefore communicate. Notice that shareability of concepts, in particular, sameness and difference, is a necessary and sufficient condition for the logical possibility of understanding the language of another. Communication and therefore sociability are a result of shareability and comprehensibility, not a condition for it. Of course, in practice it is not always possible to understand another when behavioral manifestations are lacking and there are no signs of a language (e.g., speech, signs, or writing). The empirical possibility is fulfilled when the behavior or language of another is available for observation. Thus a concept could be shareable without in fact being shared or communicated at all.

Let us consider a complex situation, one to which I shall return in Chapter 8. Granting claim [1a],

> [D]oes this show that there are ways others can discover the rule someone is following, in every case, by observation of how the speaker continues in her use of the term in question? . . . Suppose X has an odd type of sensation and calls this type of sensation an "E" sensation. Suppose there are no behavioral or other correlates of this sensation. Even if we are all present when X takes herself to have an E sensation, and hear her say that she has an E sensation on numerous occasions, surely we need be in no position to latch on to her meaning—her precise meaning, that is. We may know even that E is an "odd" sensation, but surely we need not know enough to feel that we really have any idea what sensation quality is at issue.[18]

I would respond to this objection as follows. If X speaks about *E* (and let us assume she calls it "E") I can get at the grammar of her language without initially knowing the reference of the word "E." The consistency of her word usage provides a grammatical framework so that I can comprehend that "E" refers to something, to a private sensation of some sort. Secondly, having learned X's language, if X describes *E* or says merely that *E* is not like other sensations, e.g., not an itch or a pain, I can get a sense of what *E* is even if I never have or experience *E*. For if this were not the case, then I would have to conclude further that I do not know the meaning of the term "black hole," for example, since I have never and can never experience one. In other words, a private, nonbehaviorally correlated experience can be explicated, because it is the grammar, in particular in this case the mechanism of referring, not the experience or object of reference, that is nonprivate. Suppose X has *E*, tells us on a number of occasions she has had *E*, but simply cannot describe it. Still, one cannot say that X's language is private or that her referring rule is private. It is simply that the uniqueness of *E* and its "location" as a sensation preclude either X's describing it or our experiencing it. The referent, in this case, is private, but not its entire meaning or its grammar.

But, one may counter, surely it is the case that I can never know about *E* in the way that X does, and thus I cannot know the precise meaning of *E*. This is true, but that does not lead to the conclusion either that X has a private rule for referring to *E* (she does not because I understand the rule) or (b) that I cannot have some inkling of what *E* is, e.g., it is a sensation that is neither an itch nor a pain. So *E*'s privacy does not infer that X's language about *E* is also private.

Let us consider a more difficult example which focuses on patterns of speaking.

> Suppose X has a mini-language restricted to the following four terms: "not," "this," "is," and "grive." We follow X around and X says, "This is grive" and "This is not grive" in such a way that we would be forgiven for thinking that "grive" means *green*. But actually X's rule for "grive" is such that "grive" means *green and seen by me before my death or else blue*. Of course, though X would call blue things "grive" after her death, we shall never see her do so. Now, is this story self-contradictory? . . . [One might reply]: we can teach X our language, and then she can explain what "grive" means. Can't this reply be blocked by the stipulation that X suffers from a special mental defect preventing her from learning any more words? It is perhaps logically impossible to follow the proposed "complex" rule for "grive" without following simpler rules such as our rules for "green" and "blue" also. If so, perhaps observers can have reason for thinking that if X means anything she means "green." But . . . [s]upposing the case of X and "grive" is logically possible, it is hard to see how observers could find a way of telling that X means what she does mean.[19]

This objection is both difficult and confusing. First the objection raises the skeptical question, how do we understand rules others use? My answer has been that the nature of rules is such that in principle we cannot understand rules others use. According to the example, the mini-language X uses follows the usage of English grammar. "This," "is," and "not" are all used as they would be in English. "Grive," too, functions as an adjective, like green, but obviously with a more complex and even ambiguous meaning. So I can understand X's language, even though I do not understand that full meaning of "grive." Second, if X has merely a mini-language and cannot learn more words, how is it that she has developed this complex meaning for "grive"? What is the meaning of "griveness" to X? Does X understand the meanings of, say, "death," "me," "see," or even "blue" (except as "not grive when I am not dead")? X seems to be in a catch-22 situation, for if she had such a complex idea about "grive," she could learn more concepts and thus expand her language, and we could learn about "griveness." If she does not, then the example has difficulties, for X herself will not understand the meaning of "grive."

Let us suppose that X has a brain operation, her mental defect is cleared up, and X learns a full-fledged language. After learning language she can explain to us what "griveness" means. If "griveness" means "green and seen by me before my death or else blue," then X had these concepts in mind but was unable to articulate them because of her mental defect. "Grive" was a secret word, but not an inherently private one. If X cannot explain what "griveness" was, then it is strange to say that "griveness" meant "green and seen . . . etc." to X before her operation. What would it mean so say that X had this notion of "griveness" yet could not articulate it even to herself?

V

If rule-following activities are based on rules, if rules are distinct from rule-following, if rules cannot be private, and if language-games are rule-governed activities, then at least one version of the Language-Game Thesis should concede that the notion of a rule, not a language-game, is at the basis of language and rule-governed human activities. Another version of the Language-Game Thesis, however, contends that language-games are practices, and it is the notion of a *practice* that underlies rules, rule-following, community agreements, and language-games. *"Rules do not, and cannot, define the nature of an activity . . . practices do."*[20]

To support this thesis, Wittgenstein says, for example, "'obeying a rule' is a practice,"[21] and,

Where is the connexion effected between the sense of the expression "Let's play a game of chess" and all the rules of the game?—Well, in the list of rules of the game, in the teaching of it, in the day-to-day practice of playing.[22]

Setting up rules presupposes rather than constitutes a practice so that rules are embedded in practices. So, it is concluded, rules evolve out of practices rather than the reverse.

It is indeed the case that rules and rule-following activities often in fact evolve from practices. Games in particular usually develop from interchanges which establish what counts as "going on in the same way correctly" for that particular game. I am not refuting the claim that rule-following activities are embedded in games and practices or that rules often evolve from practices or even habits of behavior. Rather, I am arguing that underlying a practice, what makes practices, games, and agreements possible, are the notions of sameness, consistency, and difference, i.e., certain primitive rules. These are very simple basic conditions underlying all human activities. Particular interpretations of these rules evolve from practices and games. But the existence of these rules makes such practices and thus interpretations of these rules possible.[23]

VI

There is another important objection to this version of the private language arguments. One could grant that one needs "sameness-establishing conventions"[24] to speak a language. But there are a wide variety of such conventions. "Sameness" (and thus "difference") is not one concept but a multiple of concepts that vary depending on the context in which they are employed. For example, the "same color red" might mean an exact shade of red, a variety of shades of red, or a family of similar shades. "The same pain" might refer to a continuing pain, my repeating identical or similar pain, or a pain of yours that seems similar to mine. The pitch C on the musical scale might refer to middle C or any other C on the piano. Are they the same note?

Similarly, referring again to the example raised in the previous section about X and her mini-language it can be argued that X's sameness-establishing convention in respect to "grive" is not the same as what it would be in respect to "green" or what ours is in respect to "green." So if sameness refers merely to disparate sameness-establishing conventions, X could develop a rule (in this case a rule for "similarity-with-respect-for griveness") that would be different from ours, and even private.

Sameness, then, is not a natural relation. Nor is sameness an "it" at all, but rather, a multiple of social conventions, practices, and habits that are necessary, albeit in different ways in different contexts, for naming and other language functions. These conventions are essential for reidentification and language, but they are nevertheless merely a plural-ity of *conventions*, some of which function in language-games. So different language-games embody different sameness-establishing conventions, and the plurality of sameness-establishing conventions reflects the plurality of languages and language-games.

However, if "sameness" is merely a series of "sameness-establishing conventions," then a number of conclusions may be derived, some of which are inconsistent with others. (a) Language could develop only in a community context where sameness-establishing conventions are agreed upon as the basis for language practices and customs. From this it follows that (1) Janet cannot develop a language in isolation, or it follows that (2) if Janet *could* develop her language in isolation from a community, this isolation would be only physical isolation, and her language would fit into a community, should we ever have a chance to chat with her. (b) Because sameness-establishing conventions are different in different contexts, different language-games and thus different languages could use conventions that were incommensurable with each other so that some languages are incomprehensible and thus not translatable and are therefore "private." From (b), (c) it could be the case that I would not be able to know whether my language rules were similar to another community's, since each language could employ different sameness-establishing conventions. (d) Worse, if Robinson could develop a language in physical isolation, he could develop a language whose rules depended on sameness-establishing conventions which agreed with those of a nonexistent community. Should this occur we could not understand Robinson should we meet him.

Conclusion (a) has been dealt with at length and refuted in Chapters 4 and 5. Conclusion (b) (from which [c] and [d] follow) hits at the heart of the arguments of this chapter, because if it is correct, then the private language problem reappears, albeit on the level of same-establishing conventions. But there is something amiss about (b). It is true that we apply terms differently in different contexts. "Going on in the same way" makes different demands depending on the particular situation in which it is used, so that there is no one-and-only-one rule for it. On the other hand, there are some "sameness" criteria or "principles" that are identical in different contexts. These include (at a minimum) consistency of application of whatever convention one is applying, e.g., the same shade of red, the same family of shades, the same number, the same pitch of C, etc. to the context in question. Moreover, sameness-establishing conventions are applications of the "principle" of sameness just as following a series (e.g., 1002, 1004, 1006, 1008) is an application of a rule. "How do I know I am going on the same way?" or "How do I know I am applying a rule correctly?" are questions having to do

154 LANGUAGE ONLY I CAN UNDERSTAND

with the *way* I "go on" (1007 will not do, pink is/is not in the family of reds), that is, the way I employ a particular sameness-establishing convention in practice. At the same time I am able to evaluate whether I am following a rule, whether I am applying a sameness-establishing convention correctly, or whether a new convention (e.g., pinks joining the family of reds) is a consistent convention, that is, whether it makes sense to try to enter pink in the red class and whether I can reuse this convention consistently so that it makes sense to me and other conventionaires (language users or color freaks), and so that I can distinguish and reasonably defend this use of a color convention from others who exclude pink from the red category. I can engage in this evaluative process because I can "stand back" from any use of a sameness-establishing convention and judge its consistency and compare it to other conventions. If I merely had at hand particular sameness-establishing conventions and lack a more general notion, I could not judge, accept, or change the conventions themselves. The fact that X can use her mini-language at all depends on her ability to "go on in the same way" and not merely on the particular convention she has adopted for "griveness." Moreover, while the sameness-establishing convention for "griveness" is not identical to that for green (although they are similar), if the former convention is used consistently, another person could decipher it from X's uses of the term.

Is there, then, a meta-concept, "sameness," a universal of which sameness-establishing conventions participate in? If I ask my children to bring home "sameness," they will be at a loss, or they would bring home some application, that is, some sameness-establishing convention. But I reject each of their examples. "What I want," I say, "is the concept or principle by which you are able to sort out and distinguish and evaluate the sameness-establishing conventions you have brought me." Of course, as Kant has taught us some time ago, the project is doomed to failure. Yet its failure is not because there are merely disparate sameness-establishing conventions and no sameness *per se*. Sameness (and consistency, similarity, and difference) are not concepts one can bring into class. Rather, they provide the conditions through which sameness-establishing conventions are developed, are understood, and are evaluated. These notions are not "somethings" but they are not nothings either. They are, if you like, the "bedrock," the ways in which we go about anything including speaking a language; they are the preconditions for our way of living. We cannot get at them because they are the basis for "getting at" and make "getting at" possible. As we argued in an earlier section, this notion, not the notion of a language-game, is the basis for language.

The notions of "rule" and "language rule" function similarly. Because "the use of the word 'rule' and the use of the word 'same' are interwoven," without being able to develop and apply patterned sound uses, there would be no language. Because consistent practices of organizing, using, and reapplying words and sentences are necessary to language, rules and rule-following are included in the notion of language. Yet it is only in developing and speaking languages, in formulating, using, and evaluating language rules that "rule" has any meaning.

To respond to the problem raised by (b), different sameness-establishing conventions are based on a notion of sameness or consistency so that rules of each individual language can be formulated, broken, and evaluated. Comparing sameness-establishing conventions of radically different communities I can understand Robinson's language even when his sameness-establishing conventions are seemingly incommensurable to mine because these conventions depend on notions that are the basis for there being conventions of any sort. X's mini-language rule for "griveness" follows a referring pattern so that others can discern the rule. While we cannot understand the extent of the reference of "grive" (but neither does X!), the rules X employs preclude the privacy of her sameness-establishing conventions and thus her language rules.

The notion of "agreement" or practice is connected with the notion of a rule, because "[t]he word 'agreement' and the word 'rule' are *related* to each other, they are cousins. If I teach anyone the use of the one word, he learns the use of the other with it."[25] Community agreements and social practices, all of which employ sameness-establishing conventions, then, presuppose the notion of a rule as the condition for making any agreements or having practices. Similarly, language-games, each of which may use different sameness-establishing conventions, also depend on the notion of a rule. The idea of a "game" depends on the notion of consistency. While different language-games can have radically different perspectives or rule-following activities, no language-game is incommensurable with others, that is, in principle, incomprehensible, because no language-game can be a *game* without the notion of a rule, a notion that precludes the logical privacy of the game in question. Finally, even the "brute fact that we generally agree" (what I have called "natural consensus") assumes a consistency in agreements and patterns of agreements. The word "agreement" and the word "rule" are *related* to each other. The use of the word "rule" and the use of the word "same" are interwoven; thus "rule" and "same" are constitutive of "brute agreements," language-games, and social practices.

VII

Another important criticism of this emphasis on the central importance of rules in the private language arguments is that this view appears to support a "rules as rails" thesis.[26] This thesis argues that language rules are determinate of their applications. According to this view, rules and rule-following are independent of human reactions, customs, and responses so that there are certain determinate applications of rules that dictate "how to go on" and "how to go on in the same way." At its extreme this thesis is a form of Platonism that there are universals or universal principles independently governing correct (and incorrect) applications of rules or uses of terms. This view is very likely contrary to Wittgenstein's description of the somewhat indeterminate character of rule-following in the *Philosophical Investigations*. Wittgenstein says, for example, "the application of a word is not everywhere bounded by rules." Or in the *Remarks*,

> How can the word "Slab" indicate what I have to do, when after all I can bring any action in accord with any interpretation? . . . How can I follow a rule, when after all whatever I do can be interpreted as following it?[27]

In §185 of the *Investigations* Wittgenstein describes a recalcitrant rule-follower who follows the series 0, 2, 4, . . . to 1000 and then begins 1000, 1004, 1008, etc. About this situation Wittgenstein says,

> We say to him: "Look what you've done!"—He doesn't understand. We say: "You were meant to add *two*: look how you began the series!"—He answers: "Yes, isn't it right? I thought that was how I was *meant* to do it."[28]

On the contrary, then, it might appear to be Wittgenstein's contention that every expression and every rule has a variety of uses and is open to a multitude of disparate interpretations in the same or different language-game.

If the "rules as rails" thesis is too strong, is Wittgenstein committed to an indeterminacy thesis about rules and rule-following? According to some advocates of this interpretation, especially some advocates of a Community View, no explanation of the use of an expression is proof against misunderstanding . . . we move towards the idea that understanding an expression is a kind of "cottoning on"; that is, a leap, an inspired guess at the pattern of application.[29]

This view allegedly is supported by Wittgenstein's statement, "When I obey a rule, I do not choose. I obey the rule *blindly*."[30] So rule-following is either "blind" habits or dispositions, or rules function like a calculus: fully complete, objective, and determinate of their applications.

The problem with both views is that neither captures what is important in the notion of a rule. While Wittgenstein repeatedly questions the "rules as rails" thesis, at the same time it is not certain that he is committed to the indeterminacy view of rule-following either. Wittgenstein claims, "A rule stands there like a sign-post . . . the sign-post does after all leave no room for doubt. Or rather: it sometimes leaves room for doubt and sometimes not."[31] A consistent reading of Wittgenstein, then, although perhaps not the only viable one, is to argue that Wittgenstein takes a middle position between the "rules as rails" and the "cottoning on" theses on the notion of a rule. There are a number of reasons to adopt this moderate position. First, Wittgenstein wants to explain the diversity of rule applications, the myriad of ways a single rule may be interpreted even in grammar. Rules can have diverse applications because the way one follows a rule is specified by the language-game in which the rule is being applied. At the same time Wittgenstein notices that rules delimit certain kinds of ways of "going on" although they do not point out The Way. This is both because the language-game in which a rule is applied limits the variety and acceptability of rule-following activities in that context or practice, and because rules are formal. Rules themselves set out the criteria for correctness, but they do not specify the content, that is, *what* must go which way, so in different contexts the same rule can be applied differently.

Gordon Baker and P. M. S. Hacker question the separation of rules from rule-following and argue that rules and rule-following are internally related. Although the term "internally related" is confusing, partly because of its checkered career in the history of philosophical use, what I take Baker and Hacker to be saying is that rules do not have the status of universal generalizations, nor do they function as hypothetico-deductive explanations. Rather, rules are internally related because acting in certain patterned ways is a criterion for "following a rule," so that an interpretation of a rule is a criterion for understanding (grasping) a rule. Conversely, the rule being applied is the norm for applying a rule correctly or incorrectly.

Baker and Hacker argue that one cannot separate "grasping a rule" from "knowledge of how to apply it."[32] Understanding a rule consists in knowing how to apply a rule correctly, and one's interpretation of a rule reflects on what rule one is following. This is at least in part true. It is not quite the case that "a rule determines its application."[33] Sometimes we merely function with applications. For example, I learn to speak a language, that is, I learn the correct uses of words and phrases and I can distinguish between correct and incorrect uses. It is then said that I know the grammar of the language even though later, perhaps, I shall learn theories of grammar. We speak; sometimes and only later (and maybe never) we learn to diagram sentences. Thus rules often function merely as rule-following applications. Moreover, a consistent but novel rule-following practice may create a new rule. But does it follow that rules and rule-following are internally related so that one cannot separate a rule (or grasping a rule) from actually applying it?[34]

Differentiating between a rule and rule-following is important because this differentiation accounts for normative and evaluative activities entailed in the notion of a rule and in rule-following. Sometimes I learn a rule first (e.g., the rule for integration in calculus) and then apply it. More importantly, I can at least theoretically separate a rule from an application of a rule, study their relationships, modify my application *or* modify the rule, study applications to extract the rule, and/or use rules to evaluate applications or interpretations. I do not want to "multiply entities" by claiming that there exists some sort of Platonic Realm of Sameness and Difference, a Sub-realm of Rules, and an everyday world of appearances or applications. But I want to separate rules from rule-following, because we actually do this so that rules are functional mechanisms which act as normative standards for directing and evaluating rule-following at least to the extent that not every application counts as "following a rule" or "following a rule correctly." It is likely that this distinction is important to Wittgenstein, too. Otherwise he would not say "there is a way of grasping a rule which is *not* an *interpretation*."

It is true that there are no "transcendent standard[s] for correctness."[35] However, one should also want to be careful not to conflate the preconditions for the possibility of rules and rule-following with a particular rule or conflate rules themselves with their applications. In the former such conflation leaves one with the conclusion that there are only particular conventions dictating "sameness of response" so that one cannot evaluate these conventions. The latter sufficiently blurs the idea of a rule with its applications so as to invite an identity of these two. Such a position, like the preceding one, precludes being able to evaluate rule-following and suggests that rule-following is dictated by conventions which themselves cannot be brought into question and thus plays into the hands of a Community View.

There is another distinction that is important to Wittgenstein, the difference between thinking one is following a rule and actually doing so. If rules and rule-following are internally related, then if I think I am following a rule, I must somehow be following a rule. This is because if rules and rule-following are internally related so that I can scarcely distinguish them, I shall also have a problem distinguishing between what I *think* is an act of following a rule from actually doing so since I cannot independently grasp the rule in question in order to evaluate my practices. Therefore, the idea that rules and rule-following are internally related blurs the distinction between thinking one is following a rule, actually doing so, and understanding the rule in question.

Rule-following is not a passive activity but involves measuring the accuracy and consistency of the application against the rule or instrument in the context of a language-game.[36] Although this may not be a perfect analogy, it is instructive because the formal character of rules allows a variety of applications, but not every application is a correct one, and one can misinterpret a rule or be misinterpreted just as one can correct oneself or be corrected. The fact that there are misinterpretations of rules, according to Wittgenstein, would indicate that there are correct interpretations as well. The formal character of rules and the way they function in language-games as guides for diverse rule-following activities allow rules to be signposts but not railroad tracks. Rules, then, operate as norms or standards for correct and incorrect applications just as, conversely, patterns of application sometimes redefine or create a rule. That rules and rule-following can relate in this normative and open-ended way without being indeterminate is because the notions of sameness, difference, and consistency "regulate" the forms of rule-following in language-games not by prescribing which track a rule will be directed, but by proscribing derailment.

VIII

An objection may be made of the project of this chapter and indeed of the book as a whole to this point. The objection is this. The Rule

Arguments as we have presented them are circular arguments. If the notion of a language includes the idea of a language rule, and if the idea of a rule and the concept of "same" are interrelated, then because concepts are, by definition, general in nature, it follows by definition that no language could be a private language. If this is the case then why have the private language arguments and in particular the Rule Arguments been discussed in such detail?

This is surely a valid criticism of the project of this essay. The Rule Arguments are in a sense "analytic" in the old-fashioned sense of that term, because languages are, by definition, not the kinds of "entities" that are private in the way in which pains or dreams, for instance, might be private. But the alleged analyticity of the Rule Arguments does not detract from the merit of examining various private language arguments and delineating this argument in particular. Whatever Wittgenstein's original private language arguments were, the private language arguments have been widely discussed, dissected, and reformulated. Because it was originally thought that these claims led to the solution of many dilemmas in epistemology and in the philosophy of mind, it is important to explore all facets of them. Moreover, in light of Community Views and the Language-Game Thesis and their interpretations of the private language arguments, it is essential not merely to question these positions but also to present alternative valid arguments showing that a private language is impossible.

What the Rule Arguments bear out is that a language, any language, by definition employs rules that guide but do not prescribe the ways in which words are to be properly and improperly used and sentences are to be constructed. By the very nature of a rule, a rule is a formal procedure for consistent application; grammar is a specific formal procedure for consistency of word function, use, and reference. The consistency and repeatability of language precludes its privacy. Therefore, one cannot construct a language, PL_c, whose rules are necessarily private. Moreover, languages such as PL_a, PL_b, or PL_d, languages whose subject matter is private phenomena, are not private languages either, because although the subject matter of those languages is private, the rules, grammar and syntax of such languages employ consistent patterns, allowing them to be translated. Even though a listener or translator of these languages may never experience the objects of reference of these languages, a translator can understand the grammar in such a way that she can understand the nature of the reference. The notion of a private language, then, either a language developed by one person, a language spoken by alien beings, or a language whose rules are logically private, makes no sense, and a logically private language is impossible.

The Rule Arguments are significant not merely because they demonstrate that no language can, in principle, be incomprehensible to others. Such a conclusion also mitigates against the viability of linguistic relativism. This is because if all languages are rule-based, and if one cannot construct a private rule, one *could*, at least in principle, understand any language, even a radically different one constructed by alien beings. The difficulty in comprehension, as we discussed in tackling the "if a lion could talk" problem in Chapter 6, is that a language is embedded in a set of practices. Sometimes these practices are so different from ours that we have difficulty understanding and thus translating the references to alien terms. These sets of practices and the language therein can be thought of as "forms of life" because they embody a whole set of conceptions, social agreements, habits, and ways of dealing with the world.

However, because "the use of the word 'rule' and the use of the word 'same' are interwoven"[37] we can distinguish between rule-following, seeming to follow a rule, and making mistakes, distinctions essential for the correct and consistent applications or uses of words. Being able to make these distinctions helps us to evaluate and interpret an alien set of experiences or different forms of life. We can do this even though a particular language embodies a strange conceptual framework, because underlying that framework are more basic notions that make such a framework possible. This "bedrock" is not the conventions themselves or even the conceptual framework underlying conventions and agreements, but rather the notion of a rule. That we can study the ways languages function and evaluate our agreements, conventions, and frameworks implies that we are not trapped within one interpretation or one way of following a rule. Because we are not inexorably wedded to our own conceptual scheme or to the linguistic conventions in which we find ourselves but can study, evaluate, and even alter them, we can at least conceive of a conceptual framework or an alien way of dealing with the world that is radically different from our own. We can even envision other possible worlds that are dramatically different from this one. If we are imaginative, we can shift conceptual frameworks because underlying each scheme is a consistency of word formation and application or reference, albeit wildly strange from our own perspective, that allows the lion's "language" to make sense within its own framework even while being difficult to translate into English.

There is one caveat. Incommensurability is not to be equated with incomprehensibility. One can only imagine other *possible* worlds and other *possible* conceptual frameworks. But there are certain worlds or conceptual frameworks that are impossible even to imagine. At least one cannot imagine a conceptual *framework* where uttering sounds randomly in the presence or absence of disparate phenomena was part of a conceptual *scheme*. What is missing in this instance is any framework or scheme at all. A so-called concept or scheme or world that is internally incoherent and inconsistent in every respect is not a world or a concept or a scheme at all. So there is a "form or life" or a "bedrock" after all, beyond which the notion of an alien concept is restricted. But that bedrock is the ground for there being any conventions, agreements, concepts, forms of life, or language whatsoever.

The Rule Arguments also challenge although do not ultimately defeat linguistic idealism. If practices as well as language are rule-based one is not forced into the conclusion that concepts are merely created by social consensus, grammar, and practices. While it is true that one can never get at a concept that is not embedded in a language or is distinct from a practice, it does not follow that that concept was formulated by that practice, but merely that any formulation is context-bound. Earlier we argued that while one can never get at the notion of a rule in isolation from rule-following and evaluative practices, it does not follow that the notion of a rule is identified with or derived from practices. Similarly, the context-bound parameters of concepts are not identical to their alleged context dependency, although it is surely the case that some concepts are created from practices. It is just that this is not an entailment relationship.

The Rule Arguments bring into question the antirealist conclusions of Wright and Kripke, but they do not conclusively defeat antirealism established on other grounds. Wright's claim that rules are indeterminate and that rule-following is a form of "cottoning on," has been decisively refuted. The distinction between the notion of a rule and rule-following brings into question Kripke's radical rule-skepticism for reasons I laid out in Chapter 5. Because practices and even community consensus are at rock bottom rule-governed, the Rule Arguments do not entail any form of antirealism, and they then do not entail the conclusion that truth-conditions are merely assertability conditions.

The negative aspect of this conclusion is that Rule Arguments do not eliminate either linguistic idealism or antirealism, or even exclude the possibility that there is a one-to-one relationship between truth conditions and assertability conditions at least in some kinds of cases. But these conclusions do not follow from the Rule Arguments and would have to be justified on grounds other than the private language arguments.

If the Rule Arguments are correct, the notion of a rule is basic to language, language development and language-games. The ways in which rules are interpreted depends on the context—the language-game or practice in which the rule is applied. Social practices and community agreements, too, play a role in the direction of these interpretative activities. But the notion of a rule is the bedrock for language-games, consensus of any sort, and social practices, all of which are rule-governed activities. So rules are constitutive of a community, social practices, and language-games.

Notes

1. Wittgenstein, *PI*, §199.
2. Later we shall elaborate on this definition.
3. See Carl Ginet, "Wittgenstein's Claim that There Could not Be Just One Occasion of Obeying a Rule," in *Acta Philosophica Fennica 28: Essays on Wittgenstein in Honour of G. H. Von Wright*, ed. Jaakko Hintikka (Amsterdam: North-Holland Publishing Company, 1976), pp. 154–165.
4. Hintikka and Hintikka, *Investigating Wittgenstein*, p. 242.
5. Wittgenstein, *PI*, §202.
6. Ibid., §258.
7. Ibid., §265.
8. A number of people have made this point, including Armstrong, "Wittgenstein on Private Languages: It Takes Two to Talk," pp. 46–62; Kenny, *Wittgenstein*, Chapter 10; Kimball, "Private Criteria and the Private Language Argument," pp. 411–416; and others.
9. See Blackburn, "The Individual Strikes Back," pp. 281–302; Candlish, "The Real Private Language Argument," pp. 85–94; and Swoyer, "Private Languages and Skepticism," pp. 41–50 for other versions of the same kind of argument.
10. McGinn, *Wittgenstein on Meaning*, p. 80.
11. This point was brought up by an anonymous reviewer of an earlier version of this manuscript.
12. See Hacker, *Insight and Illusion*, p. 222.
13. Margaret Gilbert, "On the Question Whether Language has a Social Nature: Some Aspects of Winch and Others on Wittgenstein," p. 305.
14. Gilbert, p. 307.
15. Ibid., p. 306.
16. According to Gilbert, this is because one could imagine a situation in which a person, let us call her Maude, experienced two kinds of aches, x-aches and y-aches, that Maude in private can distinguish, yet her behavior made no

distinction between these different aches, perhaps because Maude is para-
lyzed. Maude often says she is having an x-type ache or a y-type ache, "[y]et
it seems pretty clear intuitively that no one could, on the basis of the
behavioral evidence, grasp the rules for the use of 'x-type' and 'y-type' that
she is following, and so know that she has grasped those particular rules"
(Gilbert, p. 308). Gilbert complicates the Maude situation by arguing that
two people, I shall call them Maude and Mick, might both experience x- and
y-aches, sensations that have no behavioral correlates, share the same terminology, yet do not know whether or not they were using "x" and "y" in the
same way. I find this to be a strange conclusion. If Maude and Mick speak
the same language each of them can describe to the other what constitutes
an x or a y sensation. They can correct each other and each other's use of
the rule for referring. If Maude's paralyzation spreads so that she cannot talk,
indeed in fact we cannot find out if her aches are like Mick's, but this
possibility does not damage the argument for meaning-identifiability.
Maude's ache-language would be part of a secret language, but not an
inherently private one. This is because if Maude felt better and became
interested in analyzing her pains, she could explain the differences between
x-aches and y-aches.

17. Wittgenstein, *PI*, §225.
18. This objection was posed by an anonymous reviewer. It is a good objection,
    and I thank him/her for raising it.
19. Again, my thanks to the anonymous critic of an earlier version of this
    chapter for this example.
20. Hubert Schwyzer, "Rules and Practices," *Philosophical Review* 78 (1969): 453.
21. Wittgenstein, *PI*, §202.
22. Ibid., §197.
23. See David Pears, *The False Prison, Volume II* (Oxford: Clarendon Press, 1988),
    especially Chapter 14, for this sort of argument.
24. George Pitcher, "About the Same," p. 135.
25. Wittgenstein, *PI*, §224.
26. For a discussion of this view see McDowell, "Non-Cognitivism and Rule-
    Following," in Holtzman and Leich, pp. 145ff, and Gordon Baker, "Follow-
    ing Wittgenstein: Some Signposts for *Philosophical Investigations* 142–242,"
    pp. 52–55.
27. Ludwig Wittgenstein, *Remarks on the Foundations of Mathematics*, revised ed.,
    trans. G. E. M. Anscombe (Cambridge, MA: MIT Press, 1983), VI–38.
28. Wittgenstein, *PI*, §185. See also Pears, *False Prison, II*, Chapter 17 for a
    discussion of Wittgenstein's alleged Platonism.
29. Crispin Wright, 'Rule-Following, Objectivity and the Theory of Meaning,"
    in Holtzman and Leich, p. 100.
30. Wittgenstein, *PI*, §219. Hintikka and Hintikka interpret "When I obey a rule,
    I do not choose. I obey the rule *blindly*" not as a support of the indeterminacy
    thesis but rather as a conceptual point that "what goes on in one's mind
    [e.g., 'the presence of a formula'—a rule] is not a criterion whether a rule is
    being followed . . . On the contrary, rule-following has to be understood by
    reference to language-games" (Hintikka and Hintikka, p. 198). Rule-
    following is subordinate to the language-game in which the rule-following

activity occurs. In some of these games rules do function like "rails," e.g., in the game of calculus, and in other games rule-following is less determinate. So the language-game sets the stage for the kind of rule-following that is to occur in a particular context. In each game "I follow the rule blindly," that is, the determinateness of the rule-following activity is a result of the kind of language-game in question rather than a result of the rule employed, and this is "accepted" in each context.

Hintikka and Hintikka have captured an important point, namely, that rules function differently in diverse contexts, and these contexts are controlled by a language-game. From this Hintikka and Hintikka argue that language-games are primary, and rules are to be understood in reference to language-games, a thesis we discussed in Chapter 6. I have argued at length that rules, but not rule-following, are primary, and language-games are ultimately to be understood in reference to the notion of a rule. Hintikka and Hintikka, then, have cleared up an important point concerning the "rules as rails" thesis, but it does not follow from this that language-games rather than rules are most primary, since the notion of a rule underlies both determinate and indeterminate rule-following activities.

31. Wittgenstein, *PI*, §85.
32. Baker and Hacker, *Scepticism, Rules and Language*, pp. 100–101.
33. Baker, "Some Signposts," p. 53.
34. Baker and Hacker, *Scepticism*, p. 122. See Pears, Chapter 17, for a critique of Baker and Hacker.
35. Baker, "Some Signposts," p. 54.
36. Gordon Baker describes Wittgenstein's view of rules as a "rules as instruments" view. Baker depicts rules not as abstract criteria but rather as *"symbols* or *instruments* with particular uses or ranges of use." See Baker, "Some Signposts," pp. 54–59.
37. Wittgenstein, *PI*, §225.

8

"Always Get Rid of the Idea of the Private Object"

Despite our intuitive beliefs to the contrary, Wittgenstein makes the brash statement, "always get rid of the idea of the private object."[1] This statement, along with the original private language arguments, appears to force one to alter radically the notion of so-called private, mental, or psychological events. Such a conclusion is counter to the arguments developed in the preceding chapters. To review briefly the discussion in Chapters 1 and 3, one of the purposes of delineating the notion of a private language and of exploring the private language arguments was to show that the conclusions of these arguments have often been misdirected. In evaluating the Strong Private Language Argument and criticizing the Private Phenomenon Argument we concluded that the inability to verify the existence and nature of feelings or psychological phenomena such as dreams or images does not entail their nonexistence. Counter to the claims of the Private Phenomenon Argument, one can, at least in theory, develop a language whose subject matter is one's inner sensations. These phenomena may even be considered necessarily private events, at least for the sake of the argument; yet the resulting language is not a private language. In discussions of other private language arguments we have repeatedly used valid examples where a (non-private) language was constructed from phenomena that could be thought of as private, such as one's sensations. At the same time we have proved that a private language was impossible. Thus if the foregoing arguments are sound we may conclude that the denial of the possibility of a private language does not entail a radical revision in our basic intuitive beliefs that we experience and can refer to, sensations such as pains as well as so-called mental or psychological phenomena such as dreams, after-images, and hallucinations, even when these phenomena are not readily available to others.

However, we have shown merely that although a private language is impossible, the idea of a private phenomenon is not unintelligible. But there are also positive aspects of relating the idea of a private experience to the private language arguments that should be examined. What does one mean by the term "private experience?" How does this term make sense in light of the private language arguments? Are psychological phenomena private, and if so, in what way or ways? Even if it is granted that the concept of pain, for example, is understandable to more than one person, if the word "pain" refers to a purely private sensation, how can one learn from others to use this publicly understood word to identify and refer to sensations that are perceivable only to oneself? How can the word "pain" be used both on the basis of allegedly private feelings to which the word may refer and observable pain behavior, which may be reasons for saying that others are in pain? And how can one use the word "dream," for example, to refer to phenomena that have no obvious behavioral manifestations? In this chapter we shall discuss these questions.

Some philosophers use the term "psychological phenomenon" or "psychological predicate" to talk about all so-called private experiences including pains, dreams, etc.[2] I shall use the term "psychological phenomenon" in a more restricted sense to talk about those phenomena (1) that have no obvious or ordinary behavioral manifestations and (2) that have no obvious physical causes or location. Since pains and some other sensations have behavioral manifestations (although one need not manifest one's pain), and because at least pains and itches ordinarily have physical causes and physical location, they do not qualify for the term "psychological phenomenon" under my restricted definition of the expression. Second, for the sake of the argument I shall use the terms "pain," "pain sensation," and "pain feeling" interchangeably, while recognizing that they are sometimes distinguished in the literature.[3] In what follows I shall restrict my discussion to pains, dreams, and images. What I have to say should apply to other feelings and other psychological phenomena, but even if it does not, it should nevertheless contribute to our understanding of these phenomena.

I

One of the difficulties in analyzing the notion of a private experience in light of the private language arguments is to determine what Wittgenstein's position on private experiences is. The declaration, "Always get rid of the idea of the private object" could be read as meaning that so-called private phenomena, e.g., images, dreams, pains, and the like, are neither private nor objects. This view is supported by the fact that Wittgenstein sometimes talks as if language about pains, at least, is "non-cognitive avowal" language.[4] For example, he says, "So you are saying that the word 'pain' really means crying?—On the contrary: the verbal expression of pain replaces crying and does not describe it."[5] Possibly, then, Wittgenstein means that at least first-person sensation language is expressive, avowal language, and is not referential or descriptive at all.[6]

On other occasions Wittgenstein recognizes that we often talk as if we *can* refer to sensations and other so-called private or psychological phenomena. For example,

> How do words *refer* to sensations?—There doesn't seem to be any problem here; don't we talk about sensations every day, and give them names?[7] . . . The essential thing about a private experience is really not that each person possesses his own exemplar, but that nobody knows whether other people also have *this* or something else.[8]

In what appears to be an explanation of such referential expressions, Wittgenstein says further, ". . . if we construe the grammar of the expression of sensation on the model of 'object and name' the object drops out of consideration as irrelevant."[9] So terms such as "pain" refer, but "pain" apparently does not *designate* an object.[10] Wittgenstein further confuses the matter by stating, "It can't be said of me at all (except perhaps as a joke) that I *know* I am in pain. What is it supposed to mean, except that I *am* in pain."[11] If this is the case, then "I am in pain" is not a descriptive sentence. So this sentence has no truth value, since there is no instance where it could be false.[12]

Finally, Wittgenstein's animadversions against a private language may entail a denial of the independence thesis, the thesis that "it is logically possible that however similar two persons are in behavior and physical construction, still their sensations or felt quality of their experience may yet be radically different."[13] Because we talk about these experiences with words whose meanings are understood by others, we tend to assimilate reference to, and descriptions of, what might be unique private occurrences under publicly agreed-upon categories or names. So we cannot refer to any "unique felt quality" that is not accessible to others except with terms that already mean something else, and thus such references and descriptions do not capture the uniqueness of the quality in question.

This variety of apparently contrary interpretations leads one to question the consistency of Wittgenstein's position concerning private experiences and to question whether one can make sense of the notion of a *unique* private experience (or a "unique felt quality") in light of the private language arguments. In this chapter I shall argue that one can develop a consistent position about private phenomena that does not contradict the *Philosophical Investigations*. More importantly, I shall argue that one can make sense out of the notion of "unique felt qualities" without reverting to the idea of a private language. Whether or not Wittgenstein himself held this view or meant to argue this thesis is unclear, but its implications for what can be implied from the private language arguments and the viability of making sense out of private experiences is obvious.

II

When one says, "I am in pain," "I dreamed," or "I imagined," one does not expect his audience to feel his pain, to observe his dream or images, or to be able to directly verify these occurrences, because the experiences that are the subjects of these expressions are not thought of as public events. Pain feeling is not groaning, however, but it is that phenomenon as the result of which the groaning occurs. The expression "to imagine" is not to be identified with "to image." But when one says, "I imagine" it is often said that I am referring to a private "picture," i.e., an image, that one has or can conjure up. In imaging one appears to be actually "seeing," in a special way, an image or a series of images that are not visible to others. In a special way, too, hallucinatory phenomena and dream phenomena are "perceived," and it is to these phenomena that reports and descriptions of hallucinations and dreams allegedly refer.

There are two important points to be noticed in talking about psychological phenomena. First, in talking about psychological phenomena one need not commit oneself to the metaphysical position that these phenomena are mental as opposed to physical, that human beings have souls, or to any other controversial Cartesian claim about "the mental." Unlike sensations or feelings such as pains that have known physical causes, we often call psychological phenomena "mental events," simply because they physical causes are, at best, unclear, and because they need to be distinguished from ordinarily observable, publicly verifiable, phenomena.

Second, one need not say that the phenomena I have called psychological phenomena are necessarily *objects* at all.[14] The term "object" may be inappropriate to these phenomena not merely because they are not publicly observable or verifiable by others, but also because they are "observable" only when they are occurring and therefore are not privately reverifiable even by the experiencer. Such an analysis may account for Wittgenstein saying that "the object drops out of consideration." At least it is not inconsistent with the *Philosophical Investigations* to argue that way, although there are other viable and less "friendly" interpretations of this passage.

This ephemeral character of psychological phenomena is due partly to a characteristic peculiar to psychological phenomena, the way or ways we experience them. The events in dreams and images are not perceived through one's sense organs, although these experiences may seem to be very much like seeing and hearing, feeling, tasting, or smelling, because the contents of dreams and images may be very much like the contents of ordinary experiences of public objects or events. One could even argue that we do not perceive psychological phenomena at all, but rather, that we use the paradigms of sense perception to describe our experiences of psychological phenomena, because we are lacking other terms. This is a fault of our language, but a natural one that allows us to develop descriptions of, and to teach others about dreams and the like.

It is tempting to say, then, that there is a difference in the kind of perception entailed in explaining psychological phenomena. Yet we use ordinary perceptual language to talk about these occurrences. (I *saw* pink elephants; I dreamed I *smelled* coffee, etc.) Moreover, dreams, for example, have a "look alike" quality, resembling ordinary experiences. In dreaming and imagining we seem to reproduce acts of perceiving, e.g., seeing, smelling, hearing, etc., as well as objects or events that are ordinarily perceived through these acts. For example, "I dreamed that I smelled coffee while I was sitting in a cafe overlooking the Seine (which I was seeing)," etc. So the difference between sense perception and dreaming is not exactly a difference in kind of perception or object of perception. It is also in dreaming and to a lesser extent in imaging that whole perceptual events are recreated in another mode or at a level of abstraction. This view leads the philosopher Gilbert Ryle to describe imagining, for example, as a second-order sophisticated form of make-believe perceiving.[15] Ryle captures the fact that it is not a difference of perception that distinguishes experiencing psychological phenomena. It is that the whole experience itself is on another level. Ryle's analysis of these phenomena, however, as has been noted countless times, appears to question the existence of these occurrences as real events. What I want to argue is that dreaming and imagining are actual occurrences. What is unusual and interesting about these occurrences is that in dreaming, for example, we dream that we are perceiving events or objects, so that we recreate the whole phenomenon of perception, e.g., the whole action of seeing an object or of hearing a sound. Thus at least dreaming and imagining are special ways of "having an experience." The unique experiential character of psychological phenomena is connected with a characteristic often attributed to sensations and psychological phenomena, their alleged privacy.

III

In his article, "The Privacy of Pain," Don Locke distinguishes four kinds of privacy which, he argues, are characteristic of phenomena such as pains, and these distinctions are useful in discussing whether or how psychological phenomena are private. First, Locke says that something is owner-private ("o-private") if it belongs to one person or group of persons but can be shareable with, transferred to, or owned by a number of people, as, for example, a condominium is.

Second, something is logically private ("l-private") if it cannot be owned by, or shared with, others, because it is individuated by reference to the owner, as, for example, my voice or my smile is. Similarly, pains and psychological phenomena are logically individuated by reference to the person having the pain or experiencing the psychological phenomenon.[16] At least some l-private phenomena "suffer from 'identifiability-dependence.'"[17] Smiles, voices, pains, and psychological phenomena do not exist apart from smiling, speaking, feeling, imagining, or dreaming, and these activities, in turn, depend on a subject or actor, e.g., a smiler, a speaker, or a dreamer. Unlike tables and chairs, for example, these phemomena have no identity apart from the person (or animal) whose experiences they are, nor have they any "life" except when they are being "exhibited" or experienced by their "owner."

Some phenomena that are l-private, such as one's smile, may be visible to others, but I would suggest that pains and psychological phenomena differ from other l-private phenomena, because their "location" also precludes others from experiencing them or experiencing them in the way their "owner" does. The differences in ways one experiences psychological phenomena, differences we discussed in the previous section, further distinguish dreams and images from other l-private phenomena such as smiles that are publicly perceived through the five senses. These phenomena qualify for mental privacy.

Something is mentally private ("m-private") if only one person can be in the position to experience it. Here the term "experience" is used in the most general way so that pains, for instance, would be m-private if I am the only one able to be in a position to feel my pain; my images are m-private if I am the only one who can imagine them, etc. Later we shall qualify the m-privacy status of pains and psychological phenomena. But notice that it is theoretically possible for another to deceive us about them. M-privacy implies that the experiencer is in a sort of privileged position in relation to these phenomena, and "privileged access" is a fourth kind of privacy characteristic of pains, according to Locke, but the "privilege" is not, I shall argue in the next section, an epistemically favored one.

In the case of psychological phenomena such as images and dreams m-privacy is more complex. This is because the mode of perceiving psychological phenomena (e.g., dreaming) appears to be tied to the "event" "perceived" (the dream) *and* to the "perceiver" (dreamer), allowing the experiencer a peculiar privilege of access to her psychological occurrences. The "object" of psychological perception seems to be connected to the "perceiver" ("my image," "my dream") in such a way that it is linked to both the perceiver and the act of psychological perception peculiar to this experience. "'I'—'dream'—'a dream'" seem to be all of piece in such a way that the object of my dreaming is uniquely mine and could not exist apart from my having gone through the dreaming experience. This is in contrast to seeing a movie, for example, where the object of perception, the movie (but not the experience of the movie), is the same for any number of perceivers.

The thesis that pains and psychological phenomena are m-private has been attacked on a number of grounds. Wittgenstein himself says,

> In so far as it makes *sense* to say that my pain is the same as his, it is also possible for us both to have the same pain. (And it would also be imaginable for two people to feel pain in the same—not just the corresponding—place. That might be the case with Siamese twins, for instance.)[18]

What Wittgenstein may be saying in connection with pain is that you and I can have the same *kind* of pain, and if you and I share some of the same body parts, then we could and would share some of the numerically identical pains. This is grammatical ownership, because it is simply a fact that I (or my Siamese twin and I) cannot be in pain without its being mine (ours). Hence I have "logical ownership" of my pains and other psychological phenomena, because I cannot transfer my pain to someone else. So when Wittgenstein declares, "The proposition 'Sensations are private' is comparable to 'One plays patience by oneself,'" it is plausible to say that he is talking about the redundancy of that expression. The logical-grammatical ownership of pain entails a form of m-privacy such that it is redundant or even nonsense to reiterate it.

It is tempting to say that psychological phenomena are epistemically m-private, that is, because one cannot perceive the pains of another; it is logically impossible to find out what another is feeling. This position is questioned by a number of philosophers. An identity theorist, for example, could argue that if it is possible to identify sensations with recordable brain processes, then the encephalograph, a machine that records brain waves, could always reveal what one was perceiving and whether one was really feeling what one says one feels. According this theory a brain technician could always know about Smith's feelings even if she could not feel what Smith was feeling, so that Smith could not fool others about his sensations.[19] Similarly, a manometer can measure eye-blinking, which usually accompanies dreaming, so a trained technician could know that I dreamed. The possible validity of these experiments will not damage the claim that psychological phenomena are *in fact* m-private. Even if another person could find out *what* I was feeling by an encephalograph, or because I told her, this does not mean that she could feel my pain or experientially dream my dream as I do. So a qualified kind of m-privacy is preserved even under these hypothetically possible conditions.[20]

IV

A fourth kind of privacy attributable to pains, and thus to psychological phenomena, is "privileged access." There are at least two sorts of privileged access: privileged acquaintance with a phenomenon, and privileged knowledge of it. Locke focuses on the former by defining privileged access to a phenomenon "if I do not have to find out . . . [the] existence or occurrence [of a phenomenon] in the way that others do." Privileged access is also often linked to privileged knowledge. Since pains and psychological phenomena are l-private and m-private, it is sometimes alleged that I have privileged knowledge of them. So it is sometimes argued that only I know I am in pain or dreaming. If what we said about m-privacy is correct one would have to qualify the notion of privileged knowledge as the claim that no one can know my pain and psychological phenomena *in the way I do*.

In connection with privileged knowledge Wittgenstein says,

> In what sense are my sensations *private*?—Well, only I can know whether I am really in pain; another person can only surmise it.—In one way this is false, and in another nonsense.[21]

I shall argue that one can make sense of a sort of privileged access that does not entail privileged knowledge or contradict the private language arguments by examining carefully two interrelated uses of the word "know." This analysis, in turn, will shed light on the status of first-person pain and first-person psychological sentences.

Because they are m-private in the qualified way we have specified in the last section, in simply feeling pains or dreaming dreams there is a sense in which I have privileged access simply because I am the only person in the position to experience these phenomenon as I-am-feeling-pain or I-am-dreaming-a-dream. Do I not, then, know I am in pain, or have knowledge of my pains in ways you do not? Is this first-person acquaintance privileged access or "knowledge" about pain? Let us see.

According to Wittgenstein, "You learned the *concept* 'pain' when you learned language." Before a person, R, has learned a language, R probably had pain sensations of which she was aware (i.e., R felt pain), but she could not be said to have any form of acquaintance or knowledge of them. It is not until R learns language that R first finds out what pains are, how to distinguish them from itches, dreams from waking experiences, etc. After R has learned language R can employ two, albeit related, uses of "I know I am in pain." "I know I am in pain" may mean that I am having an experience, that this experience is a pain experience, and I am acquainted with it. In this use of "know" (let us call this k_1), "I know I am in pain" is redundant or identical to "I am in pain." It is only redundant because (a) pains are identifiability-dependent, (b) R knows language so that she can sort out her identifiability-dependent phenomena, and (c) having learned what pains are, R does not have to find out she is in pain in the way others do. (a), (b), and (c) appear to imply the thorny thesis that once R knows what pains are, she cannot be wrong about the identification except in borderline cases, e.g., between pains and itches, dreaming and daydreaming, etc. These borderline cases are not problematic, according to this view, however, because when I learn language I also learn to distinguish these as "borderline cases." We shall question this thesis in a later paragraph.

There is another use of "I know I am in pain" that is not obviously redundant. For after R has learned language (and therefore can recognize that the preceding use of "I know I am in pain" is redundant) R might also say, "I know I am in pain," where R means (a) that she understands the difference between pains and the absence of pain, pains and itches, or pains and dreams of pains, and (b) that R recognizes what she is now experiencing as a pain. Let us call this use of the term "know" k_2.

Interestingly, these two uses of "know" can also apply to knowledge about/of so-called non-private phenomena. For example, "I know I am seeing a page" can mean, "I am having a sensation of a phenomenon, I am aware I am having it, and I cannot doubt that." Or, "I know I am seeing a page can mean "I recognize *that* what I am seeing is a page from a paper on private phenomena. It is not a table." The difference between "I know I am in pain" and "I know I am seeing a page" appears to be in the fact that another person cannot correct my identification of a pain while she can correct my identification of a page. This alleged fact accounts for the erroneous conclusion that while "I see this page" is a true or false descriptive statement (since it is publicly verifiable and correctable), "I am in pain" is not (allegedly because it is neither publicly verifiable nor correctable).

The source of this error is a confusion between two uses of "know": k_1 and k_2. When I make an assertion about my present feeling state (e.g., "I am in pain"), there is a sense in which I just *do* recognize feelings without criteria, although this occurs only after I have learned what pains are. Similarly, I can recognize a page merely by acquaintance after I have learned what pages are. There is a sense, then, in which I use the expressions "I am in pain" and "I see a page" as assertions, without criteria or justification. But, "to use a word without justification does not mean to use it without right."[22] The "right" derives from my having learned a language so that I can name and recognize what I directly experience. Moreover, like "I see a page" describes what I am seeing, "I am in pain" is also descriptive of the *kind* of feeling I am experiencing. When asked, I can describe my feeling and you can correct my identification. ("We call those itches.")

Does not the distinction between k_1 and k_2 leave us with a problem? For it appears that sentences such as "I see the page," "I am in pain," "I know (k_1) I see a page," or "I know (k_1) I am in pain" are first-person sentences that can only be true and never false. Since these sorts of sentences cannot be false, according to some interpretations, they are either redundant or nonsense. I think, however, that one need not be forced into this conclusion. This is because first-person sensation sentences and first-person psychological sentences of the type k_1, "I am acquainted with my pain," are possible to utter only after I have learned language. This is true even for our isolated friend, Susan Crusoe, who develops her own language. Susan can have pains and dreams, and see trees, flowers, and pages. It is arguable that Susan can *recognize* and perceptually distinguish them much as other animals make such distinctions. But Susan cannot name these phenomena or attach meaning to sounds until she has developed a language. Therefore primitive or prelinguistic utterances in the form of "I am in pain" or "I see a page," should they occur (although one cannot imagine a prelinguistic Susan using so many sounds in the presence of a single sensation), are momentary avowals or signals expressing the occurence of a sensation, feeling pain, or seeing a page. But these signals do not even ostensively define these sensory phenomena until Susan learns a language, because while Susan may repeat the same signal ("I am in pain") when a similar phenomena reappears or is sensed again, there is no guarantee she will do so. The connection between "pain" and the feeling of pain is neither deliberately made, consistently applied, nor correctable. Prelinguistically, these expressions have no connection with identifying a pain or knowing one is in pain. Any so-called knowledge of my pain or my sensation of a page elicited even merely by my own acquaintance with these phenomena can occur only after one has learned language. After that, "I am in pain" is often used as an avowal ("Ouch!") or signal, but it is also used in other ways as well.

Therefore, the expression "I am in pain" is (1) an assertion of my present feeling state, and/or (2) a description of a sensation that can be indirectly verified by asking me to describe the pain feeling (a description of which I am capable only when I have learned language), and/or (3) an avowal, an expression.[23] (1) is possible only after I have learned a language and can identify my sensations and psychological phenomena. (1) of course is the allegedly problematic interpretation because it appears to be unverifiable. But (1) is indirectly verifiable and can be erroneous just as (2) is. This is because I can make assertions about a feeling or a psychological phenomenon only after I have learned language, so my references may be erroneous (I mixed up pains and itches) or not follow "accepted practice" of other language users (I misused a word). (1) is distinguished from (2) (and therefore distinguishing k_1 from k_2 is a useful if not altogether clear-cut distinction) because k_1 and k_2 are different uses of the expressions "I am in pain" and "I know I am in pain." (1) is a form of association where "I am in pain" as an identification of a sensation implies I know I am in pain, that is, that "I know I am in pain" is redundant. My identification may be wrong, but not the fact that I am feeling something. In the use k_2, "I know I am in pain" is a descriptive sentence inviting amendment, correction, or affirmation.

If one replaces "I am in pain" with "I see a page" the results are similar. In the latter case "I see a page" is:

(1) an assertion of what I see, and/or,
(2) a description of what I see, and/or,
(3) an "aha" sentence ("Page!").

(1) can be as problematic for "I see a page" as it is for "I am in pain," for it could be that I misidentify what I see (I point to a page but I am hallucinating about elephants). In that case (1) is also indirectly verifiable by my describing what I see (e.g., "I see a large grey page with a trunk and tusks"). Finally (1) can be false, when I am confused or lie about what I see. ("I see a large thick grey object but others say I am pointing to a black-and-white flat thing.") But the falsity lies in the identification of the object, not in the fact that I am seeing something.

Turning to "I know I see a page," this sentence is redundant for a linguist in the sense of k_1, after he has learned a language and can identify his perceptions. But it is redundant in the same way that "I know I am in pain" is redundant. Moreover, as I suggested in the preceding paragraph in discussing "I am in pain" or "I see a page," "I know (k_1) I am in pain" is not infallible and is indirectly verifiable, because I can misidentify my sensations or misuse a word.

There is another sense in which neither "I know I am in pain" nor "I know I see a page" is redundant—that is, when "I know I am in pain" (k_2) is used to mean "I recognize this sensation as a pain sensation" or "I recognize that object as a page." Pains seem messier because they are felt only by the speaker. But, I am arguing, this is because of the m-l-privacy of feelings and psychological phenomena, because of the peculiar way psychological experiences are experienced, and because of their "location," not because of the privacy of *language*. Therefore, postlinguistically, "I know am in pain" or "I know see a page" describes what I am experiencing. In the latter case error is possible when I misname, misidentify, or misdescribe what I experience. So in the use

k_2, "I know I am in pain" and "I know I see a page" are not redundant or always true (infallible), or even jokes.

It might appear that (3) avowals have prelinguistic meaning. For example, we assume that a baby's crying means that she is in pain. But the assumption that crying is an expression of pain is a postlinguistic interpretation of the baby's noises. This is not to imply that we should ignore such sounds because the baby in question does not understand pain. In fact, the strong physiological identity between babies and adults and the postlinguistic testimonies that crying often signals pain strengthens our belief about the meaning of the baby's avowals. The point is that (a) the baby does not make the connection, although she often stops crying when the pain symptoms are relieved, and (b) it is only after we have learned language that the avowal-pain connection makes sense, just as "aha" signals "Page!" only in certain linguistic contexts.

To spell out the notion of "privileged access," because feelings and psychological phenomena are l-private and m-private in the sense that no one else can perceive or experience my pains and psychological experiences in the ways I do, it would be a contradiction to say that someone else felt my pain or dreamed my dream in the way that I do. It is also possible that I can experience pains or psychological phenomena without being aware of them. Or, at least, I can "block out" pain, for example, with other diversions. But, conversely, I cannot be aware of sensations and psychological phenomena without experiencing them. Therefore one's sensations are not distinct from one's being aware of them in the same way that verbal reports, for instance, are distinct from their subject matter. For what would it mean to say, "I have a pain, but I don't feel anything."[24] This allows Wittgenstein to say that in one sense "'I know I have toothache' means nothing or the same as 'I have toothache.'"[25] I have privileged access to my psychological phenomena and pains (1) because no one can experience these phenomena in the way I do and (2) because I could not be aware of my dream, for instance, without dreaming (although I can dream without being aware of that dream), while it is always possible to be in pain or to be dreaming without others noticing it.

A more precise definition of privileged access, then, would be: I have privileged access to a phenomenon if it would be a contradiction to say that anyone else had experienced the phenomenon in the way I do such that I could consistently and meaningfully but not infallibly report experiencing the phenomenon. Privileged access, however, is literally limited to the "privilege of access," and only when I have learned language can I be said to enjoy that privilege. Knowledge of one's psychological phenomena is neither privileged nor infallible. My pains and psychological phenomena are in some senses private, but the concepts of these phenomena are not. So I can be acquainted with my pains and report my experiences only when I can speak or understand language. I can make mistakes about what I experience privately, others can learn that I am in pain or what I dreamed, and they can correct me. So privileged access is not an epistemic privilege.

V

Turning to Wittgenstein's famous statement, "Always get rid of the idea of the private object," we see that what Wittgenstein writes in full is

(The temptation to say "I see it like *this*," pointing to the same thing for "it" and "this.") Always get rid of the idea of the private object in this way: assume that it constantly changes, but that you do not notice the change because your memory constantly deceives you.[26]

Wittgenstein is declaring that we should not "worship" a so-called private object as an inalienable indubitable phenomenon to which one has a privileged epistemological status and which serves, therefore, as a proper logical starting place for philosophical analysis, language development, and a source of epistemic certainty. Therefore it is not inconsistent with this statement to conclude, as we have argued in the preceding section, that the privacy of pains and psychological phenomena is a limited experiential sort of privacy and as such has no epistemic value. The "object" in question is an ever-changing phenomenon dependent on being experienced by someone for its existence and dependent on language for its identification, conceptualization, and definition. Sensations and psychological phenomena are not epistemically privileged, nor is the term "object" in the traditional sense of an empirically reverifiable phenomenon appropriate in referring to them. Any sort of glorification of private objects, then, does not lead to the grandiose philosophical conclusions once thought.

VI

Let us return to the independence thesis: ". . . that it is logically possible that however similar two persons are in behavior and physical construction, still their sensations or felt quality of their experience may yet be radically different." In principle the possibility of "radically

different felt experiences" cannot be denied. Yet if one cannot conceptualize unless or until one learns language, and if that language is not a
private language, then one has only publicly developed accessible referential and conceptual mechanisms. How, then, can the *language* I use
to describe allegedly unique felt experiences, being a public language
employing non-private concepts, refer to or describe the unique quality
of the peculiar experience in question? This position has been labeled as
"weakly verificationist" because while one can refer to private experiences so that the private language arguments are not verificationist
about reference, these arguments may not be verificationist about
sense.[27]

To give an example of what is at stake with a weakly verificationist
position, suppose there is a person, S, who is the only person to
experience a particular sensation. If the private language arguments are
verificationist about sense, the words S uses to talk about his sensation
are publicly understood. Let us suppose that S experiences this sensation only once, and during that sensation period he utters the sound
"glub," which heretofore was never used in S's language. Does the
sound "glub" signify? Can it be used as a name and have meaning so
that it can be understood later? Since "glub" must have a public meaning in order to be understood, according to this view, either "glub" is a
synonym for another already meaningful word in S's language, or it is a
nonsense syllable. So S might experience a unique sensation, but either
he is not able to talk about it, or if he does, he must use words or
synonyms of words that already have meaning, depriving his description of whatever was unique about glub.[28] On the other hand, if one can
conceptualize about qualitatively unique sensations, one should also be
able to speak about such sensations. But then, according to the foregoing, no one else could understand what one was talking about. So, it
is argued, this possibility is precluded by the private language arguments.

This thesis (that the private language arguments are verificationist
about meaning or sense) is consistent with a Community View of language. If meanings of words and expressions are determined by dispositions, habits, and/or social agreements about what words *should* mean,[29]
then when S, the person who experienced glub, tries to describe what
may have been a unique private experience, it is argued, we would
translate that description into terms we all understand. We might decide, for instance, that S's description is a description of an itch. Notice
that in fact we often do this sort of translation, particularly when

children describe their experiences, both private and non-private. According to the verificationist-about-sense interpretation of the private language arguments and a Community View, this is the only way we can get at S's experiences. So even if S has had a peculiar experience, or if the "felt quality" of some of S's experiences are unique, because S can only describe his experiences in terms whose meanings are publicly agreed upon, the rest of us will never know about S's experiences in the way in which S experiences them, and S will have difficulty himself distinguishing their uniqueness.

The impossibility of the independence thesis seems to be supported by what is purported to be Wittgenstein's analysis of how one learns sensation language, or at least, how one learns language about pains. In brief, Wittgenstein said that when a child cries we introduce the concept "pain" to her by teaching the child to replace the crying with appropriate words such as "I am in pain."[30] We introduce the word "pain" to a child for her use in referring to experiences she had previously noticed and that she had expressed but which she could not talk about. Hence, reference to pain is introduced by replacing behavioral reactions with words that one may use to refer to experiences that are the basis for these reactions. But how does one know that a child's crying means that she is in pain or is hungry? What assurance have we that our descriptions of her behavior are correct and that the terms we introduce correctly refer to the kinds of phenomena she is experiencing? Or, better, why does one presuppose that these descriptions *are* correct most of the time?

What underlies one's assumption that crying in a baby, for instance, means that the baby is probably in pain, is the prior similarity of response to certain stimuli. What is implied is that because there is a basic similarity in our reactions, one understands the expressions and movements of others, and hence means of communication in the form of language can develop. This is not to say that a long time ago people met and decided that their reactions agreed. Such a "gathering" could not take place unless one's reactions to events already coincided with the responses of others to similar events.[31] What is being suggested is that language is based on a "consensus of reactions,"[32] a version of what Kripke calls the "brute fact that we generally agree." Such alleged natural consensus, according to this theory, grounds the conditions for our assumption that crying, for example, is a natural expression for the sense experience of pain. The problems with this sort of conclusion have been thrashed out in Chapters 5 and 6.

Without denying that in fact our reactions and our sense experiences do agree most of the time, one need not appeal to this fact to explain private reference and to exonerate the independence thesis. This is because a "consensus of reactions" theory is not an adequate description of language and language learning, nor does it explain how we refer to phenomena that have no obvious behavioral manifestations or where behavioral manifestations are not necessarily criteria for the phenomenon in question. Therefore, that account does not preclude S's uniquely referring to his glub. Nor does it preclude the rest of us from understanding about S's unique experiences, from learning about glubs, and even empathizing with S when he is feeling glub, even though we have never felt anything like glub ourselves.

When one learns language, in particular, when one learns to name, what one learns is not merely a series of particular references from which generalizations about pains or glubs develop. Rather, one learns *how* to name and refer. One of the reasons Wittgenstein attacks the "idea of the private object" may be because, he argues, one does not and cannot learn *language* merely from sound-object ostensive associations in the absence of any sort of associative rules.[33] In brief, as we argued at length in Chapters 3 and 7, making ostensive definitions depends on a prior understanding of pointing or some other associative methodology as a rule for associating sounds with objects in order for the ostension to take place. When I have learned *how* to make ostensive definitions I can then name and refer to a variety of similar and disparate phenomena by way of this associative mechanism. But without "learning how," I cannot even primitively refer to my own individual sensations.[34]

Our friend S, having learned language and having learned how to refer, can deal with a new sensation. When he experiences what heretofore has never been spoken of or written about, S can identify the sensation as something new by comparing it to other sensations, and he can create a new word to denote it, "glub." Notice that this helps, too, to explain how we can refer to psychological phenomena that exhibit no concomitant behavioral manifestations. One learns to refer and identify. One learns to refer to sensations that have correlative behavioral manifestations, and one learns to refer to those sensations without considering their behavioral concomitants, thereby learning how to refer to so-called publicly unverifiable phenomena, a technique we then employ in talking about images, dreams, and even unique sensations.

Second, following Wittgenstein's claim that "the use of the word 'rule' and the use of the word 'same' are interwoven,"[35] when S speaks, even in trying to refer to his unique feelings with a new word, whatever words and expressions S uses and for whatever reason, S uses them consistently. So we can get at the pattern of S's use of the word "glub." When we converse with S he can explain to us that glubs are not like dreams or hallucinations (although S has dreams or hallucinations of glubs), they are not itches, etc. Notice it will not help S to try to simulate the glub he feels, because we are all immune to such feelings. But through various descriptions and comparisons we can get at what S means by "glub," and we can get an inkling of what it would be like to feel such sensations. Moreover, if S experiences a glub only once, if S has a language, he can name this sensation and give it meaning ("the sensation I felt once"), and the rest of us can understand that meaning even though we have no evidence to verify the use of the word and even if S experiences no new glubs with which to check his reference. These are the sorts of tasks language in fact actually does, especially in poetry and fiction, which is to refer to, describe, or create descriptions of unique experiences and events that may occur only once or only to one person or only in the imagination. Nor do we merely "translate" such descriptions into terms whose meanings are already agreed upon. Rather, the notion of a rule and its essential role in language allow the creation of new terms and expressions that have their own, heretofore unknown, meaning and may refer to the "unique felt quality of our experiences." What is precluded is nontranslatability of glubness in the more general way such that no one but S could understand that term. All such new terms and expressions are, in principle, comprehensible by other language users even when the phenomenon referred to by a term is experienced only once by one person (and perhaps then only in her imagination), so that reference to the phenomenon is never available for verification.

Notes

1. Wittgenstein, *PI*, Part II, p. 207.
2. For example, Hacker in *Insight and Illusion*.
3. See Norton Nelkin, "Pains and Pain Sensations," *Journal of Philosophy* 83 (1986): 129–148.
4. See Hacker, *Insight and Illusion*, Chapter 9, for a complete description of this view.
5. Wittgenstein, *PI*, §244.
6. See, for example, Kenny, *Wittgenstein*, pp. 182–185.
7. Wittgenstein, *PI*, §244.

8. Ibid., §272.

9. Ibid., §293.

10. Peacocke, "Reply [to Gordon Baker, "Following Wittgenstein . . .]: Rule Following: The Nature of Wittgenstein's Arguments," pp. 84–86. See also Christophe. Peacocke, "Critical Study: Wittgenstein and Experience," *Philosophical Quarterly* 32 (1982): 162–170; and Philippa Foot's critique of Peacocke, "Peacocke on Wittgenstein and Experience," *Philosophical Quarterly* 33 (1983): 187–190.

11. Wittgenstein, *PI*, §246.

12. See Hacker, *Insight and Illusion*, Chapter 9, on this point.

13. Blackburn, "How to Refer to Private Experiences," pp. 201–202.

14. Ibid., p. 202.

15. Gilbert Ryle, *The Concept of Mind* (New York: Barnes & Noble, 1949), Chapter 8).

16. Siamese twins, if they share parts of the same body, must also share some of the same bodily feelings. Hence, neither the movements of the bodily parts they share nor all of their sensations are l-private. But, one might say, these are l_2- and m_2-private, because they are not shareable with anyone other than the twin to whom one is physically united.

17. Hacker, *Insight and Illusion*, p. 246.

18. Wittgenstein, *PI*, §253. From this Anthony Kenny once argued that according to Wittgenstein, it is merely *de facto* the case that one cannot feel the pain of another. So pains, at least, according to Kenny, are neither l-private nor m-private. However, this view appears to belie our ordinary intuitions that only I (or my Siamese twin and I) can feel my (our) pain or dream my (our) dream. See Kenny, *Wittgenstein*, pp. 185, 188–189.

19. D. M. Armstrong, "Is Introspective Knowledge Incorrigible?" *Philosophical Review* 72 (1963): 419–420.

20. See Oscar Hanfling, "What Does the Private Language Argument Prove?" *Philosophical Quarterly* 34 (1984): 468–481.

21. Wittgenstein, *PI*, §246.

22. Ibid., §289.

23. See Hacker, *Insight and Illusion*, pp. 251–264.

24. Kurt Baier, "Smart on Sensation," *Australasian Journal of Philosophy* 40 (1962): 64–65, and "Pains," in the same volume, pp. 1–5.

25. Ludwig Wittgenstein, "Wittgenstein's Notes for Lectures on 'Private Experience' and 'Sense Data,'" ed. R. Rhees, *Philosophical Review* 77 (1968).

26. Wittgenstein, *PI*, Part II, p. 207.

27. Various philosophers have suggested this in one way or another, including especially Blackburn, "How to Refer to Private Experience," pp. 211–213. See also Stewart Candlish, "The Real Private Language Argument," pp. 85–94; James Hopkins, "Wittgenstein and Physicalism," *Proceedings of the Aristotelian Society* 75 (1974–75): 121–146; Charles E. Marks, "Verificationism, Scepticism, and the Private Language Argument, *Philosophical Studies* 28 (1975): 151–171; and Swoyer, "Private Languages and Skepticism," pp. 41–50.

28. See Blackburn, "How to Refer to Private Experiences," pp. 202–203.

29. I have argued in Chapter 4 that such an interpretation is unjustified in view of the private language arguments.

30. Wittgenstein, *PI*, §244.
31. Rush Rhees argues this point this way:

> I am not saying, "People see that their reactions tally, and this makes communication possible." That would assume considerable understanding and language already. The agreement of which I am speaking is something without which it would not be possible for people to see that their reactions tallied or that anything else tallied. We see that we understand one another, without noticing whether our reactions tally or not. *Because* we agree in our reactions, it is possible for you to teach me something. . . . The consensus of reactions is in this sense prior to language.

Rush Rhees, "Can There Be a Private Language?" *Proceedings of the Aristotelian Society* (Suppl.) 27 (1954): 87.
32. Rhees, "Can There Be a Private Language?" p. 87.
33. See Wittgenstein, especially *PI*, §27–38.
34. See Chapter 7 for an elaboration of this argument.
35. Wittgenstein, *PI*, §225.

9

Conclusion

This book has shed light on issues raised in the *Philosophical Investigations* by presenting viable private language arguments and by attacking immoderate conclusions that are said to follow from these arguments. The private language arguments draw up important implications about language, but they do not entail a radical revision of one's intuitive beliefs about truth, mind, or even language itself. This book, then, is aimed at discouraging exaggerated interpretations of the later Wittgenstein and setting the stage for continuing philosophical analyses that take seriously the non-privacy of language.

The importance of the private language arguments cannot be overestimated. These arguments have altered our way of approaching certain philosophical issues. In particular, we have had to rethink the epistemic contribution of philosophical programs that begin an analysis with what is allegedly perceived or known with certainty and attempt to derive other truths about the world or ourselves from that starting place. As a result, we have had to reformulate our views about language and the relation of language to thought and to the world. However, the kinds of conclusions that can be derived from the private language arguments have sometimes been misrepresented. Because of questionable explications of the private language arguments, some philosophers have attributed to Wittgenstein views about private experiences, the relation of language to the world, and even about the origins and development of language that are not in keeping with the careful and moderate positions expressed in Wittgenstein's later philosophy, particularly in the *Philosophical Investigations*. Representative of these questionable conclusions are the Private Phenomenon Argument, Community Views of language and truth, Wright's antirealist conventionalism, Kripke's rule-skepticism, and even the interpretation of Wittgenstein as a physicalist by the Language-Game Thesis. Wittgenstein may have held one or more of these views, but their problematic nature as representative of

187

Wittgensteinian thought makes them suspect as viable interpretations consistent with the intent of the original private language arguments and the corpus of Wittgenstein's later writings taken as a whole.

The private language arguments have to do with the privacy of *language* and not with the privacy of the subject matter for a language or with the absence of a community. So it does not follow from the private language arguments that a private psychological experience makes no sense. Conversely, the existence of psychological phenomena does not entail that they play a central role in language development. Even if one denies that psychological experiences are unique, infallible, or indubitable, this does not thereby preclude their nonexistence. To question an idiolectic basis for the foundation of language is to argue that the ground for language and facts about the world cannot be derived from such a starting place. This conclusion does not entail a rejection of realism, it is not a proof that there are no truth conditions for factual sentences, and it does not follow that language evolves only from social practices. Wittgenstein may be a skeptic, and surely there are passages that support such a position. But it is doubtful that Wittgenstein is skeptical about the role of intentions and mental states in rule-following, because he virtually dismisses mental states as playing an active role in grasping a rule. Moreover, the central focus on the notion of a rule in the *Philosophical Investigations* implies that it is highly questionable that Wittgenstein is a rule-skeptic.

The private language arguments, then, do not commit their advocates to a specific set of conclusions about the nature of mind, beliefs about the world, or even to rule-skepticism. Rather, as I have suggested, these arguments are created largely to dispel the validity of certain intriguing but nevertheless rigid views about the topics, intriguing because they promise Truths and rigid because they prescribe exactly how one is to proceed in order to deduce these Truths. The private language arguments show that the notion of language is embedded in our way of thinking and acting and that languages are complex. So the simplicity promised by philosophical analyses such as Hume's is achieved only by begging the question of the enterprise itself. Nevertheless, the communitarian flavor of the arguments does not entail a whole-hearted commitment to any of the Community Views. Community Views confuse the fact that human beings are social creatures with a more parochial claim that language development depends solely on community agreements. This latter position is too narrow to account for the normative and self-evaluative character of language. Similarly, the private language arguments are not antirealist. To say that one cannot learn the meaning of an expression or the truth of the fact it expresses merely from introspection from my own experiences does not entail a denial of truth conditions. Rather, it requires us to reexamine what is entailed in a nonidiolectic context. To question the traditionally ascribed relationships between rules, rule-following, and truth-conditions does not imply that these relationships do not exist. Instead, it calls for another analysis of these connections.

What is to be gleaned from the private language arguments? In summary of the variety of points developed throughout the book we may conclude:

1. No language can be formulated merely from ostensive definition or private ostensive definition.

2. Because the notion of a rule is the basis of language, and because rules cannot be private, the idea of a private language is an absurdity.

3. Linguistic relativism is, in principle, an untenable thesis, although in fact it may be the case that the practices, ideas, or language of a particular community are not understood by others.

4. Linguistic idealism, the claim that "essence is created by grammar," cannot be derived from the private language arguments.

5. So physicalism, epistemic realism, and even moral realism are viable philosophical theses, although they cannot be definitively established merely from the private language arguments.

6. Wittgenstein's term "form of life" is best understood as descriptive of collections of practices, agreements, and language-games that distinguish a particular culture, a society, or even a species.

7. Underlying the notion of "form of life" is the "bedrock" of human activities, the notion of a rule.

8. Turning to the question of private phenomena:

> A. The conceptual "equipment" that enables us to comprehend, explicate, and understand these phenomena is linguistic; therefore the linguistic analysis of our private experiences is not private.
> B. Sensation words name sensations. "Pain" refers to pain-feeling. Words talking about psychological phenomena refer to those phenomena.
> C. Feelings such as pains and psychological phenomena such as dreams and images are in some senses private phenomena, that is, they are o-, l-, and m-private.
> D. These phenomena are "identifiability-dependent" phenomena.
> E. One has "privilege of access" to these phenomena, that is,

pains, dreams, and images are inaccessible experientially to others in the sense that I cannot experience your pain or dream your dream in the way that you do. But,

F. Feelings such as pains and psychological phenomena such as dreams and images are not epistemically private.

G. It is logically possible that the felt quality of each person's experiences may be unique and that words referring to such felt qualities have unique reference and unique descriptive content while being understood by others.

H. The claim that "You learned the *concept* 'pain' when you learned language" does not exclude the possibility of experiencing unique felt qualities or being able to explicate this.

I. Therefore, the nature of the self, while understood only when one is linguistically adept, is not thereby devoid of individuality or privacy.

9. Finally, the conclusion that rules are constitutive of language-games, social practices, and community agreements is not meant to neglect the important role of these practices in human activities and, in particular, in language. Sets of these practices create forms of life, and some of these forms of life are radically different from others. What I have focused on is the "bedrock" of language, language-games, and human practices. The notion of a rule is that bedrock on which language-games, customs, institutions, and thus forms of life function in a multitude of ways to create, develop, and change that most important human phenomenon, language.

Name Index

Subject Index

[NOTE: The subject of this work is the nature and consequences of Wittgenstein's private language arguments as he explores them in *Philosophical Investigations*. So the terms "Wittgenstein," "private language," and *Philosophical Investigations* are not indexed.]

193